MY CORNER OF THE WORLD

MY CORNER OF THE WORLD

Life Lessons from the Classroom

A. J. Bucon

Copyright © 2018 A. J. Bucon.

All rights reserved. This book or any portion thereof may not be reproduced or used in any manner whatsoever without the express written permission of the publisher except for the use of brief quotations in a book review.

Printed by IngramSpark, in the United States of America.

ISBN: 9781732895003

First printing, 2018.

500 MILE PRESS

Wheeling, WV, 26003

www.ajbucon.com

DEDICATION

To Mom, for teaching us all about love and caring.

LESSONS

	Preface	1
1.	Deep Breaths	5
2.	Welcoming Committee	11
3.	The Green Grass	19
4.	Superman	33
5.	The Metamorphosis	45
6.	Taco in a Bag	57
7.	The Scrapfolio	69
8.	Standards of Doubt	85
9.	In the Palms of Our Hands	107
10.	Snowflakes of Glue and Love	121
11.	Midterms	139
12.	Cheese	151
13.	Git 'Er Done	161
14.	Seeds	175
15.	Into the Reflecting Pool	187

Preface

In the summer of 2017 I began a year-long journey back to a period of time that carried great significance in my life professionally, socially, and spiritually. In 2012 I returned to my alma mater Central Catholic High School, home of the Maroon Knights, after teaching at Ralph L. Fike High School in Wilson, North Carolina, for twenty-one years. The change and self-discovery of that first year at CCHS in Wheeling, West Virginia, remains a transitional point in my life during which I reaffirmed my beliefs about teaching and the importance of connections with others.

During the previous summer in 2016, I heeded the call of an inner voice which beckoned me to write. I began my blog called *Time and Space* a week or so after school had ended that year. The first moment I shared on my blog related my heartfelt ruminations surrounding the West Virginia Single A State Baseball Championship, the last baseball game colleague and friend Jamey Conlin coached before losing his life to cancer the next fall. I entitled that post "Life Lessons in the Rain" in the hopes that I could convey my insights about community, about life, and about love through what I witnessed as life unfolded a remarkable story during the emotional experience of that one game. While writing my blog, I found a voice which yearned to be heard.

After a year of examining life through *Time and Space*, I found that people genuinely appreciated the insights about my own life and gained some perspective which they could apply to their own. I was proud of developing a dedicated following for my blog, but eventually my posts became less frequent as I began to invest time in an exploration of my thoughts and feelings surrounding the year I returned to CCHS. Through my personal writing I hoped to develop a larger narrative, one that began in the spring of 2012 and concluded well over a year later. I was not convinced that I could connect all of the moments and prayed my instincts would guide me to where I needed to travel.

Many people, both in North Carolina and here in Wheeling, served as inspiration throughout the experiences I recall in this book. In Wilson I have so many friends and colleagues who influenced me to become the teacher I am today, the one who returned home to Wheeling with a level of confidence developed through the years we spent together. Here in Wheeling I have found a new set of friends and colleagues who have taken the time to show the "new kid" the ropes when he came back home. While the road was a challenging one during a period of transition for all of us, I am grateful to be part of the staff here at CCHS. Both groups of teachers labor in a special and sacred profession which is equally challenging and rewarding. Throughout nearly thirty years of teaching I have been absolutely blessed to have encountered so many remarkable students in North Carolina and West Virginia. I especially have to thank the CCHS Class of 2013 for making that journey with me that year. Including all of you individually in these pages proved to be an impossible task, but please know that I envisioned all of you as I wrote about our year together. Your name may not be mentioned in the pages, but your spirit is still there between the lines.

As I wrote this book, I chose to examine times in my life that were wonderful experiences as well as those moments which were challenging for me professionally and personally. Throughout the book I include students who represent a cross-section of the young people in my classes. I also include many of the friends and colleagues who have been a part of my life throughout my nearly thirty years of teaching. My descriptions of both groups of people are intended to be thoughtful and loving recollections. I share these memories because they are the ones which are important to me and have never had any intentions to characterize anyone in an unfavorable light whatsoever.

Several people were aware I was writing this book and provided tremendous feedback throughout the process. Kathy Proctor, a friend and fellow teacher from Wilson, provided much needed impetus at the outset of the book as she believed I had a thoughtful story to tell. Betsy Knorr, a young teacher at CCHS who started the year after I arrived, made up for the lack of proximity between Kathy and me and offered confirmation that what I was writing was a genuine portrayal of myself and the people included in my pages. My childhood friend and confidant Jodi Anthony Proietti was there down the stretch with honest feedback and critiques. I will always be grateful for that March weekend at Hilton

Head with Jodi and her husband Vic when Jodi sat up with me all night reading the first half of the book over a bottle or two of wine. I knew then that I would have the fortitude to finish what I had started. Finally, I have to recognize my mom Betty Bucon who patiently awaited each chapter upon its completion while respecting the closed door to my study. She always kept telling me I was so talented. I know a mother has to do that, but her words inspired me when I was too tired to continue.

Here I am, ready to introduce "my corner of the world" to anyone who might be interested. I hope that you find some story which inspires you in these pages. I hope that you learn what I came to understand back in 2012 and 2013 and what I eventually rediscovered while writing this book. We all experience change throughout our lives which leaves us in a world we never anticipated. We may want to retreat to places of comfort, we may regret the decisions that brought us here, and we may see the road ahead as one which is shadowed in doubt. Yet we have a golden opportunity, one which allows us to make this world in which we find ourselves a little bit better than it was before we arrived.

A.J. Bucon

1
Deep Breaths

I am akin to every other person in the world who takes a periodic deep breath, gathering strength before diving into a situation I would rather not experience, remaining stalwart when I am facing failure or success, venturing down new paths, or encountering tragedies. A solid deep breath provides me that extra latch to secure my emotional baggage until I find the footing which typically arrives much later rather than sooner. I slowly exhale that same deep breath, acknowledging this breath is no longer the same as it once was. With this release is the expulsion of joy, relief, sorrow, anxiety; the exhalation of that deep breath is so much a part of truly living.

What is it that connects the breathing and exhaling? Instinct? Choice? Perhaps something more? Breathing is the instinctive process of all living creatures. We do this walking through life, preparing our meals, laboring at our jobs, loving our fellow man, laughing or crying at the daily news, sleeping and dreaming at the end of each long day. Deeper breaths exist as a conscious effort we make in anticipation or preparation for that which is forthcoming. For me, these deep breaths are the times in my life for which I do not always understand the significance until much later, sooner if I am lucky, perhaps never should the fates determine the meaning remain perpetually elusive.

My life is a constant—almost conscious—exchange of deep breaths and exhalations. I am not so different from other people, but I wonder if by saying I am just like everyone else, I am missing something more intrinsic. Have I gone from moment to moment, reveling in the excitement, surviving the despair, never to actually see each moment as part of a larger picture? Am I taking these deep breaths without realizing the significance of each one, choosing to paint them all the same, ignoring the value of each as I lump moments together in a collection of the unexamined aspects of my own life?

I can recall the anxiety of moving back to West Virginia after spending over twenty years of my life teaching at Ralph L. Fike High School in Wilson, North Carolina. Returning to my alma mater Central Catholic High School in Wheeling was to be the pinnacle moment in my life during which a hometown son, one who had no choice but to move away to follow his dreams, returns home more confident and more cognizant of traditions and values, prepared to bring a slice of the world he has experienced back to his original community.

I climbed the three flights of stairs up to Room 301, the classroom in which I would teach that year, recalling those younger days when I could leap two and possibly three steps at a time. Thirty years had left me with neither the strength, the flexibility, nor the desire to even attempt that type of athletic feat. A different type of emotion supplanted

My Corner of the World

my adolescent desire to avoid the anxiety of winding through the hallways as I hoped to arrive before class in time to complete the homework I had forgotten the previous night; now a longing to enter the next room in my teaching career, a new world to create for both me and the students I had yet to meet, spurred a slower, more deliberate ascension up that maroon-tiled staircase. The principal Julie Shively had handed me a collection of keys, sending me up to the corner room where I had spent three years speaking Spanish under the tutelage of Señora Papagan.

An internal laugh, one I should have anticipated, soon manifested itself as an outright chuckle once I entered the room. I guess it is impossible to truly escape the past, particularly when the tangible aspects of it remain exactly the same in my memory as well as in reality. The small desks, those metal single desks, the slide-under-from-the-left desktops, the ink and lead colored pencil slots, the huge cavernous holding area for stacks of books underneath the smooth seats. Is it possible they are the exact same ones in which I sat over thirty years ago? I laughed aloud as I slid into the diminutive confines of one, gazing up at the adjacent chalkboard awash with chalky remnants of notes from the end of the year that had been erased into artificial clouds on the green painted slate stone. I must have chosen the same place where I sat decades ago in Señora Papagan's class, for as I looked up to the inch-thin cork strip across the top of the chalkboard, I saw the words "CHI-CHI" solidly printed in ink. Was I really having memories about that word and how my classmates all giggled about saying something so dialectically profane, anxiously watching for Señora Papagan's stern reaction to even its casual utterance? "Alberto!" she would shout, a smile eventually developing at the side of her mouth while I blushed under the watchful gaze of Jesus hanging from the gargantuan cross on the far wall. I sat there reminiscing the drudgery of the preterite and the imperfect tenses, the clank of the penny jar whenever anyone spoke a word of English, the joy of the off-color skits we presented to one another in our broken Spanish. "A room can't do that to you, can it?" I wondered, shaking my head while wandering towards the windows along the back wall.

The view from Room 301 mirrored my life at that point. I glanced down at the courtyard, once a place where senior classes took a picture for the inside cover of the yearbook. I viewed the construction, the massive holes being dug for a renovation on the courtyard, the demolished sidewalks splayed as fodder for jackhammers which would rattle the windows of my classroom the entire year. I looked at the dome of the cathedral which pristinely blended into the blue sky surrounding it, untouched and detached from the chaos of progress which emanated from the courtyard below. Both unattached and attached at the same time. Two pictures yet only one story. The loud, annoying transformation of the past in the hope for a calm, compelling future, the cyclical change of life in all its glory.

After taking a deep breath, I exhaled.

A moment.

So here I am, quixotically journeying through my memories of the distant past as they become prologue to the life I am living now. What do I hope I will find? Perhaps I will discover those life-affirming moments that happen in an instant and those that transpire over the course of time, those moments in which what I do as teacher, as guide, as listener, or as friend create unique connections with my students, parents, family, and colleagues, or even those moments when I have overcome obstacles to my personal growth and my vision regarding education. These moments offer some perspective about the purpose of life, the ways in which we treat one another, and the growth we experience together as human beings in a crazy, joyous, indifferent, and, at times, dysfunctional world.

Taking a deep breath.

Exhaling.

2
Welcoming Committee

It is rare in our lives to be offered a fresh start, particularly after spending so much time in one place, living one set of experiences that may or may not mirror our new ones. This fresh start can be empowering and frightening at the same time, and so I fall back on the tried and true, the choices that have brought me the most comfort when dealing with transition. As a teacher I always take comfort in the yearly tradition of "setting up my room" for the upcoming school year. However, this year was different; I was starting from scratch, not so much with the room itself but with my personal and professional life. I wanted to maintain an open mind, to avoid judging people, to refrain from comparisons to my life in North Carolina, to embrace the newness of it all, and, most importantly, to enjoy the moment.

One day after I had returned to Room 301 as a Central teacher rather than a Central student, I began the creation of my new corner in this world. The three-story flight of stairs proved no less difficult to climb as I carried a box of my favorite teaching treasures saved from my years at Fike High School. Balancing the box in my left arm, I pulled open the heavy fire door to the third floor where for the first time I met Jamie

Campbell, a history teacher with a friendly smile who strolled down the hallway from her room at the opposite end. Jamie, the social studies chairperson, another former Central student turned teacher, emanated a warm energy, the kind you would want to find after wandering through the dark in the cold winter.

"Hi," Jamie said as I threw open the door. "Mr. Bucon?"

"Please, call me A.J.," I smiled, hoping to move past formalities as soon as possible.

"I'm Jamie Campbell. Jamie. Can I help you with that?" she asked as she offered her outstretched hands. "Do you have any other boxes you need brought in?"

I shook my head as I put the box down on a table near the door. "No, I'm good. My niece Emily is coming soon to help me set up my room. Thanks though."

"Oh, that is so nice of her. Emily is so sweet." Jamie followed me into the room. "I am so glad to have you here this year." I smiled, nervously saying I was happy to be back at Central, then we continued with our introductions, casually shifting into small talk about both our past teaching experiences, our lives beyond the world of education, and our thoughts about the upcoming year. Little did I know at the time that we would grow into two friends who lived and breathed Bruce Springsteen, two colleagues who would become kindred spirits when life at CCHS became an asylum, and, most importantly for me, with Jamie as my navigator, two adventurers in a frantic quest during one of the darkest periods of my life.

"Hi, Mrs. Campbell."

My Corner of the World

"Hi, Emily," Jamie responded to Emily who walked through the door carrying two more boxes. "A.J., I will let you get back to fixing up your room. Don't forget we have faculty mass tomorrow morning. Let me know if you need anything."

With a smile I walked Jamie out. "Thanks for stopping by so soon. That means a lot. I'll see you tomorrow."

Turning on some Counting Crows on the CD player I had brought, Emily and I jumped right into work. Of course, I gave Emily all of the hard jobs, beginning with scrubbing the student writing from the desktops and washing the cloudy remnants of notes off the chalkboard. I unpacked my treasures from the boxes and began organizing my desk in the corner.

I wondered how Emily was feeling about all this. I had spent seventeen of her early years growing up living in North Carolina, watching her become a high school senior from afar, talking to her on the phone, "liking" her family's pictures on Facebook, and enjoying her playing basketball when I visited at Christmas. Now "Uncle A.J." was here in Wheeling, here at Central, here at the outset of her senior year. If I were to put myself in Emily's place at the time, I would probably be mortified at the prospects of my uncle becoming my teacher, totally uneasy that he would possibly embarrass me or even cramp my style. I am sure I did that on more than one occasion, but I also hope I brought some style and magic to add a special touch to senior year for Emily and her friends.

Emily and I spent the morning making this old, dingy room livable. Once she finished scrubbing the desks, Emily began to put them in straight rows facing the front chalkboard. I hate straight rows in the classroom and use them only sparingly: for testing, for speeches, and for Spartan Roman classroom control. In my twenty years of teaching, I have found having twenty or thirty teenagers continually facing me to be a bit overwhelming and not particularly my style. "Um…Emily, I really don't do straight rows very often."

Emily reacted with an interesting mixture of her dad's exhausted "tell me what the hell you want then" stare and her mom's encouraging "Oh, that's cool. Let's do something different" outlook. So I jumped in to help her as we pulled the desks out of the rows and moved them into sections of six or eight desks, forming a u-shape, more of an elongated semi-circle which was perfect for conversations in which we would share our thoughts, tell our jokes, and say our prayers without having to turn our heads to see one another. The focus was going to be on them, on seeing one another. It was cramped, but it worked. Emily perked up, a slight smile coming to her face, "Yeah, I like this."

I continued unravelling my teaching self as we decorated the room with posters that had adorned my walls in North Carolina for years. It was an eclectic collection of personal favorites mixed with sentimental hand-me downs from other teachers. L.L. Cool J leaned on the back wall with a book in his hand encouraging us to "Just Read;" Michelle Pfeiffer and her posse from the movie *Dangerous Minds* stood to the left of my teacher desk prepared to pointedly remind students that "there are no victims in this classroom;" and superheroes from the Marvel Comics Universe commanded the space above the side chalkboard. Emily professed that the guys in the class were going to love that last one.

My Corner of the World

Once Emily and I finished mounting the unfolded tracts of writing modes and language as well as the prayer and motivational placards, I eventually retrieved my favorite wall adornment, placing this close to my teacher desk on the wall to my right, smack dab beside Jesus and the smartboard. A huge poster-sized photo collage of Fike students I had taught over twenty years simply deserved its place there, for they were my past, the students who suffered through my early years, those who laughed while attempting my crazy ideas, and the ones I would not easily forget. This collage is part of my story much like the forthcoming collage to which I would progressively add a few more candid snapshots year after year at Central, filling it with students I had taught and those who had touched my life. Emily and I spent some time looking at those faces of students spanning fifteen years of my life in North Carolina. I could not tell at the time, but hopefully Emily found someone who reminded her of herself there.

As we were tidying up for the day, satisfied that the room was good-to-go until students began to fill the desks in a few days, another person arrived to see the new guy in Room 301. Greg Sacco was a blast from the past, an oldie but goodie, one of the few remaining older than I "old school" teachers.

"Coach Sacco," I said, crossing to shake his hand.

"A.J., you can call me Greg," he offered. I would eventually default to the name students all used to call him back in the day, the name which had stuck around for decades: "Sac."

I remember when I lived in my second story apartment back in Wilson. An older woman, a retired school teacher, lived in the apartment below mine. She was a pleasant and cordial lady, her hair in an unsettled coiffure and her walk a slow and deliberate gait, almost as if she were in a constant state of recovery, a veteran from too many years teaching beyond what her mind and body could tolerate. I had tremendous respect for her, someone who had spent her life in this noble profession; I had always hoped that her worn countenance did not mirror the spirit that remained inside.

Sitting across from Sac, I had the same respect for him. I saw the same fatigued appearance, and I wondered whether he had reached the point of being endlessly tired. Sac asked me if it seemed Central had changed much since I was a student. I told him how the carpeting on the floors was nice and the chapel looked wonderful, but other than that—the maroon lockers, the hospital green brick walls, the dusty rooms, the diminutive desks—everything seemed the same. He chuckled, informing me of the obvious that some of the teachers had grown a little older now. Sac and I reminisced down identical paths as we explored my recollection of teachers and classes from the time I was a student to his own memories of Central's history and tradition. I could have spent the rest of the afternoon there with Sac, listening to his anecdotes, hearing about the changes at Central and in Wheeling. I would have future conversations during which he would feel comfortable talking even more about the students, the traditions, and the challenges of change. Sac would retire two years after I arrived, sadly passing three years after that.

Making the transition back to Wheeling and to Central is a choice I would come to question continually since I opened that door years ago. Change is never easy, so when I ended my tenure at Fike and chose to return to Wheeling, I felt as if I were cutting off part of myself, leaving behind aspects of my life that had tremendous value to me: a wonderful school, colleagues, friends, and family. Of course, we never truly leave those parts of ourselves behind as we move on to different paths in our lives. We carry who we are, who we love, the choices we make and those we avoid, the actions and inactions of our lives into the future with us.

I accomplished more that day than simply moving some newly cleaned desks around the room and mounting some posters on the walls. Three distinct and thoughtful people welcomed me to my new world, making me comfortable with appreciating the first step of my future while allowing me to embrace parts of my past, the more recent ones, and those of a season decades preceding. Sac rose to head slowly back to his room down the hallway near Jamie, first telling me he was glad to have me here and that it was going to be a good year. Emily gathered our belongings, I turned out the lights, looking back at what we had accomplished, and I admitted that returning to Central might have been a good choice after all.

3

The Green Grass

While we taught together for nearly twenty years, Felissa Battle was always one mobile trailer away or several classrooms down the hall from me but never far from my heart and soul. Spending an extended period of time anywhere will allow anyone to find that one person who is your partner in crime, your confidant, your nurturer, your truth-teller, and your friend, a person who knows your heart because you both have traveled a long road together.

As I was considering the move back from North Carolina to West Virginia, I found myself sitting in a student desk across from Felissa, hoping for her to make the decision for me, to give me tacit approval for the life-changing choice I was about to make. Felissa would never do that though; she knows the value of making decisions for yourself. She was not without words of wisdom though.

♦

In preparation for the upcoming student orientation the next morning, I sorted through papers in my new room at Central. Jamie Campbell stopped by to remind me that it was time for the faculty mass down in the chapel. This was going to be odd for me. Issues swirled throughout my brain as the anxiety of meeting more new people again jumped to the forefront. Why was I here? What will this be like? How will I be perceived? And now—faculty mass at nine o'clock in the morning. Questions. Questions. Questions.

Jamie and I walked down the stairs to the first floor chapel which was already filled except for the first row in front of the altar which remained open as the entire faculty had situated themselves in the pews behind it. I may have been frustrated that we had not arrived earlier to secure a back pew for a better view to begin my recognition of faces, but I was probably more embarrassed as we appeared to be the two students arriving to class the moment the bell rang. Frank Przybysz, my chemistry teacher from thirty years ago, stood to the side strumming his guitar as the small gathering prepared to sing the opening hymn. With discreet smiles and nods quietly floating back and forth among the faculty, Jamie and I made our way to the front pew where I picked up a bulletin which listed the hymns, scriptures, readers, and celebrant, then I continued to read it over half a dozen times to avoid making eye contact until much later. So much for continuing to embrace my new beginning.

◆

"OK, Felissa. This is what I have," I began as I unfolded a sheet from a yellow legal pad, a single piece of paper now torn and crumpled from the paralyzing indecision about the choices I was making in my life.

My Corner of the World

Felissa smiled warmly, pushed the papers she was reading aside, then leaned in to consider my obsessively generated list of pros and cons for staying in North Carolina versus returning to West Virginia. Felissa knew me, recognized my challenges of living so far away from family, the frustrations of a long school year, my conflicted life of choices and concessions. "Let's hear it," she chuckled, knowing what was coming while still offering her warm and undivided attention.

I rattled through both sides of my list, comparing and contrasting thoughts and ideas just as I would ask any of my students to do. I had nearly made a Venn diagram but had not reached that level of obsession. *In hindsight* I know that the answer was already there, but *in that moment* Felissa knew that I struggled putting my ear to the voice of my heart. I felt I had accomplished more than I ever wanted not only inside and outside the classroom at Ralph L. Fike but also in my personal life in Wilson, this North Carolina city situated at the intersection of I-95 and US264. Returning to my alma mater in Wheeling, West Virginia, had been a long-term dream despite my having created a truly special situation at Fike as a teacher surrounded by a great support system of colleagues, friends, and family. The balancing of my two worlds, my past and my future, had generated this stoppage in time which allowed me to reconcile who I am and who I will always be.

"Well, you will be missed here." Felissa began. "I will miss you. I really think we all expected you to leave at some point to go back to West Virginia."

"I think I always knew that in the back of my mind, too. It just never seemed to be the right time until now. This is such a hard decision though."

Felissa nodded then slowly and methodically asked, "Are you really going to be OK with giving up everything here? Starting all over again? Meeting new people? A.J., that seems to be such a hard thing to do." When you open yourself to others by sharing your memories, personal experiences, and questions about life, those people are afforded the opportunity to offer insights that can truly guide you, the types of insights you can trust. Felissa knew how much time and effort I had invested in the English Department, the student activities like basketball and volleyball, the senior projects, and the entire school community at Fike. She knew that while those efforts and personal rewards would always be mine, they would remain a garden of seedlings and mature flora which would continue to grow in my absence. Felissa knew that meeting new people was an experience neither of us truly enjoyed as we both valued the calmness of familiarity and commonality. Felissa knew the challenges I would face and the possible ways in which I could rise to the occasion or succumb to the pressure.

Questions of the heart are always spiritual in nature. Arriving at this stage of my life, I had many unanswered questions, proverbial roads I had not travelled, and aspirations to engage another world with a book full of wisdom and experiences to guide me this time. Some unknown factor, some story perhaps, one I needed to write, was calling me. "I know," I told Felissa, "but maybe a new start is something I need to have in my life right now."

My Corner of the World

◆

Monsignor Ostrowski, a thin, gray-haired man, entered the small chapel on the first floor of CCHS from a back door behind the altar as the faculty softly sang the opening hymn with Frank Przybysz's guitar accompaniment. We were a small group, but there were plenty of us to fill the intimate gathering spot with music. My angst over my recent move, my relocation, and my new job slowly began to dissipate as I began to embrace that I was in a different place, specifically a spiritual one. Monsignor Ostrowski has always been a priest to select perfect passages and psalms for the moment, for the times and places we are in life, including themes that he expresses beautifully in his homilies. I learned that morning he is also very direct when people wander off their higher purpose in life, avoiding the course God intends.

Any serenity that I relished during that opening hymn was short-lived as the nature of the readings, responses, and Gospel, messages about serving God, about sacrificing, and about loving one another as a family in Christ became lost in a subtext and tone I had not expected. Monsignor vocally smacked the sections about *service*, about *sacrifice*, and about *love* with a hard rhythm, underscoring the significant parts with a pointed finger which brought back uncomfortable moments from parochial grade school when an old nun would burn the fear of God and eternal damnation into my young soul for some transgression I can no longer remember. Concerned about catching the gaze of Monsignor Ostrowski, I quickly turned my head to my left where Jamie sat stiffly on the pew beside me, my eyes widening as I felt his oncoming reprimand during the homily. Jamie looked at me, widening her eyes as well, clenching her jaw while forcing a small, uncomfortable smile only I could see. We both turned back to Ostrowski, prudently.

As I sat there during the homily, I recalled teacher "kick-off" activities I had attended back in Wilson County: the county-wide assemblies with motivational speakers, the superintendent speeches discussing student achievement and test scores, and the student entertainment. I had never experienced something quite like this mass as activities at the beginning of the year were meant to generate excitement (even though some were excruciatingly tedious and overblown spectacles of nothingness). I continued to listen to Monsignor's demand for more *cooperation, kindness,* and *better communication,* directly reminding the staff seated in the pews to remember our purpose: to educate students and to be role models for the students and community. The homily became a frank, thoughtful, and stern mandate, one not directed at me but one which affected me nonetheless.

After the service as people slowly left the chapel, some silent, some whispering, and some even smiling, I waited behind with Jamie to absorb what had transpired during the homily: a calling on the carpet, a come-to-Jesus meeting, a lecture from Daddy. Jamie and I paused to look at each other in silence until I whispered while attempting to respect the sanctity of the chapel, "What the hell was that about?"

♦

"You are OK being *here,* right?" Felissa inquired. "I mean, if you choose to stay, that wouldn't be so bad, would it?"

"I don't know. I'm just tired, Felissa. It has been a long year, and I am just not happy anymore."

My Corner of the World

"Not happy with what?"

I was uncomfortable with this part of the process, laying out reasons I was ready to make this change. Yes, it is easy to claim "confidently" that I had accomplished so much at this school, that I was ready for new challenges; this can be subterfuge for underlying issues, dirt I would rather just keep swept under the carpet. Decision-making of this sort is best done with my eyes wide open though, so I "vented" to Felissa the issues I was having, many of which she had already heard but those that clearly had simmered long enough to begin bubbling back to the surface.

In education, as in most professions, the day-to-day challenges tend to generate angst as a teacher becomes more seasoned. As someone who constantly wants to make things better, to create a near-perfect situation, I become frustrated with change, change for the sake of change, change under the guise of progress, change dictated by behind-the-curtain entities who do not truly "know" me, my teaching philosophy, or even the student population. Most people who know me will admit, with my forthright blessing, that I have control issues, so in a situation where I must relinquish control or in which I had no control from the outset, I flounder and become frustrated, having to delve deep into my patience reserves to move forward with my own vision while serving the wishes of the larger group. This creates conflict within myself as I want to be liked, I want to be appreciated, and I want my ideas to be heard. I can and have taken a backseat to divergent directions and am perfectly fine doing so as long as everyone sticks to the plan, following the designated and approved map we all agreed to follow. Maybe just a touch of control issues.

So Felissa sat back, crossed her arms, and let me uncork my vintage bottle of critical discontent: the principal who said one thing and did another, colleagues who did poor jobs yet continued teaching, the paperwork on top of paperwork, the forthcoming Common Core and the high-stakes testing which accompanied it, the dictates from the county and the state, student apathy and poor attendance policies, the chronic complaining thrust my way as department chair with the hope that I could solve any and all problems. God help me and my judgmental and, at times, self-righteous attitudes. Felissa just smiled and agreed. As I said earlier, we know each other.

The most important characteristic of the venting process for me is that the person to whom you "uncork" must allow you unfettered and uninterrupted time to pour out every last issue, then, with your permission, he or she can then comment or even challenge what you have said, offering advice if asked. The two of us had this routine down pat.

"So, A.J., I get all of that. I do. I mean those issues are always part of this job. I have a question though."

I nodded in agreement, realizing that this is what I needed. Whether or not I would be able to authentically answer her is up for debate.

"You are painting this picture of where you want to teach, why you want to go back to Wheeling, and *everything* you say is totally understandable. How do you know that the grass is really going to be greener there? I mean, what if the situation isn't what you expect? What if you have regrets once you make this *huge* change in your life?"

My Corner of the World

I looked out the window by Felissa's desk, searching for an impossible answer in the unknown. "Yeah, good point. I really don't know," I whispered, shaking my head, answering as authentically as I could.

◆

I left the faculty mass with unanswered questions, quietly climbing the flight of stairs back to my room to continue my now half-hearted preparations for the upcoming year. The unanticipated dampens my enthusiasm quickly, reducing the impetus for creativity and purpose. I just wanted a fresh start, so how could I keep the surreal moment of returning here as untainted as possible?

Less than an hour later, Julie Shively, the second year principal, sent an email to all staff that we would be meeting that afternoon in the cathedral for our first faculty meeting, one meant to address all lingering issues from the previous year. As I sat at my computer reading the email, tension pulsed behind my eyes and flowed down my neck. "Oh, God," I mumbled, forcefully massaging my temples with my index fingers then slowly and firmly pulling both of my palms down the front of my face in order to gain perspective while attempting to wipe away my anxiety. "This is not happening."

Honestly, I do not recall why we met in the cathedral. The inside was under construction just as the outside courtyard had been for the majority of the summer. As I walked through the front doors, I dipped my finger into the holy water which glistened even in the sparse midafternoon light of the huge church, genuflecting while making the sign of the cross. Pews were moved so that tiles could be replaced and seats refurbished, creating an unsettled environment for a mass much less a faculty meeting. Chairs had been placed in a circle near the rear of the cathedral where pews had been moved, allowing a theater-in-the-round experience, except for the fact that we were all actors as well as audience, both participants folded uncomfortably into one.

The meeting felt as if I had walked into the O.K. Corral with everyone ready to take sides in a battle not quite as important as the eternal conflict of good vs. evil but one fairly significant in the lives of the stakeholders gathered in this quiet, secluded, and sacred locale. Despite my already having spent two days here, I did not feel as if I had truly become acquainted with each person individually, so this would prove to be an interesting meeting. Jamie sat to my left as she had done during the morning mass. I noticed Sac situated across the circle, flanked by senior staff, several teachers I had as a student when I attended Central. To their right, moving back around the circle towards Jamie and me, were the younger staff members, not new teachers, but older ones, the ones who had taught for years but had not yet acquired the senior staff nomenclature. Then to my right sat the administration: Julie Shively, the newly-hired assistant principal Becky Sancomb, Monsignor Ostrowski, and Vince Schmidt, Superintendent for the Diocese of Wheeling/Charleston. Above us all the vaulted cathedral ceiling led towards the marble altar at the front of the pews with the tabernacle situated yards behind it. Jesus bowed his head on the cross above the tabernacle with angels and saints to each side, all quiet observers sitting in the light emanating from the colorful stained-glass windows adorning the area surrounding the altar.

My Corner of the World

I knew I was going to sit quietly throughout all of this, conscious that there were unresolved conflicts that had festered throughout the end of the previous school year and on into the summer. Talk is good though; I firmly believe in controlled discussions during which people can say what they need to say and, hopefully, listen to one another with compassion and understanding. Monsignor Ostrowski began with a prayer to ask God for guidance and wisdom.

Vince Schmidt is an imposing yet curious-looking man, towering a good six foot five and wearing round Harry Potter style glasses; he emanated a sense of calm control from his chair where he sat with his arms crossed. Schmidt appeared annoyed with this meeting but was ready to do whatever he could to move the staff back on course. He began by sharing his thoughts on the challenges of change, and, echoing Monsignor's homily from earlier that morning, the idea that we as teachers are "here for the students." Schmidt brought up Common Core, explaining that Julie Shively was simply doing what he had asked all principals to do throughout the Diocese, which was to utilize a common set of standards as a guide for developing our instruction. As teachers we occasionally must check our students for understanding and comprehension; however, if Vince were our "teacher," he would have had a hard time reading the "class" which sat in front of him. Some fixed their eyes on Vince, nodding attentively; some crossed their arms, sitting with a thin veiled look of contempt in their eyes; some folded their hands, resting politely in their seats with a blank expression on their faces; and some "heard" him, referring periodically to a written list of concerns as they rehearsed what they planned to add when afforded an opportunity.

When Vince finished, Monsignor announced the discussion stage, the "venting" of all relevant issues so that the staff could move forward from this point. Jamey Conlin, a passionate red-headed math teacher and baseball coach who was a just few years younger than I, sat up then began, "Thank you for having this meeting. Now, before I get started, I want to say that I don't want to offend anyone with any of these concerns. I do care about the students and just want to make Central a better place." Monsignor and Vince nodded, Julie leaned forward to hear what she could have heard sitting back in her chair, Becky looked at me and I at her, while others sat up awaiting Jamey to throw the first pitch. When someone says, "I don't want to offend anyone," expect offense. I would discover much later that Jamey Conlin was more complex; while he could be argumentative, challenging, and petulant, he was also known for his kindness, his honesty, and his love for teaching. Jamey was tapped to be the "voice" of the others. If anyone could explain the issues, if anyone could fix the problem, Jamey was your guy.

According to the 90's hit comedy, *Seinfeld*, when a person "yada-yada's" during a story, this tends be a part he or she does not think is necessary, something that has no purpose or contribution to the overall message. Jamey loved *Seinfeld* and would often quiz people with phrases or names from the show, so I am sure he would understand this next part.

Red-faced and intense, Jamey began in mind-numbing detail: "This is all about communication or lack of it"—yada-yada—, another person joined in about "harshly worded emails or those that never received a response"—yada-yada-yada—, more people added "confusion about Common Core and how it is a terrible idea"—yada-yada—, then finally—"the school has a negative atmosphere." I do not "yada-yada-yada" my way through this part because the details are not important; I "yada-yada-yada" because the details mirrored many of the same reasons I had listed to Felissa last spring when I considered making this move. I empathized with the emotions on display here: the frustration, the mistrust, the confusion, the anxiety. The meeting wound on for over an hour, revisiting all of these issues yet again with the misplaced hope that they would not reoccur simply because a higher authority had instructed everyone to move on.

♦

Leaving the cathedral after my deja vu experience, I felt the trajectory of where my choices had taken my life landing heavily on my chest. My mind searched for answers, for guidance about how to adjust to this new yet disturbingly familiar environment I had entered, an environment I had lived in another time and place in a previous chapter of my life. The last part of my talk with Felissa returned as the afternoon breeze blew behind me, memories of the green grass back in North Carolina surrounding the parking lot at Fike moving to and fro in my memory.

"A.J.," Felissa smiled, awakening me from my long gaze out the window beside her desk. "You are going to follow your heart and make the choice that is right for *you*."

"I hope so, but what if you are right? What if the grass isn't greener there?"

"Then you will do what you always tell me to do. Keep remembering that you cannot change every part of the world all at once. Just focus on making your corner of the world the best it can be."

As I hopped in my Explorer to head home to regroup, I turned on some Springsteen to spark the fire of excitement again in my soul. Choices are available to me every day of my life: I can choose to regret, choose to complain, choose to rise above all naysayers, and choose to do my best regardless of the circumstances. My corner of the world may be a small place, but it is by far the best place to start planting seeds for the future, those which will need nurturing of the soul, protection from elements of derision, extra space for unexpected growth, and a nice spot for the sun's warmth. My corner of the world can be a place which grows more seeds of hope, love, wisdom, and understanding, seeds which have the potential to spread to other faraway lands, to other corners of the world.

Deep breath. Tomorrow would be here soon.

4

Superman

The raucous student body filled both sides of the blue and gold gym bleachers for the afternoon pep rally at Ralph L. Fike High School, a pep rally meant to generate some enthusiasm for that night's basketball game. For as long as I can remember, pep rallies included numerous school cheers, a cheerleader dance routine, the fight song from the band, a few student speeches, and a skit or competition among the classes. On this hot North Carolina afternoon, the warmth from the sun and the pulsating energy from the students pushed any cool air out of the gym, leaving me, my student dance team, and our opponents sweating atop the Golden Demon logo at half court while the student body president announced the upcoming dance competition.

Weeks earlier my student Brandon and his friend knocked on my classroom door to beg me to help them in the dance contest. Initially I laughed aloud, graciously thanked Brandon for the opportunity, and explained that I had no desire to attempt the dances that "kids do" nowadays. I am a sucker for self-promotion, but even this was a bit too much for me; I was a middle-aged, slightly overweight white guy who had to keep a watchful eye on his energy reserves. Brandon was quite persuasive though, earnestly offering to come to my room at lunch to teach me the dances we would be doing. I acquiesced because this *is* what teachers do when asked. Brandon, his friend, and I gave up our lunches, working endlessly to help me find the beat in "Crank That" while crash-coursing the moves for *Soulja Boy* to have me ready for the competition. For the next two weeks, I tossed aside my inhibitions, listened to Brandon and his friend, sweated entirely too much before afternoon classes, and learned *Soulja Boy* and *The Stanky Leg* from my student.

◆

Emily and her friends, the maroon and white clad senior class, entered The Great Hall, the recently remodeled cafeteria at Central which had earned the name as a result of either the swankiness of the décor or the fact that a huge, nearly life-sized crucifix overlooked us from the wall. The senior knights sat in groups close to the front of the stage but several tables removed from the microphone. We teachers sat along the side walls on higher bar-stool type chairs near their accompanying tables where we kept a watchful eye on the students as we reviewed what we were going to say.

Julie Shively, a former Air Force officer, had an ordered affectation as she politely welcomed the students back from summer break, reviewed the schedule, and then immediately handed the microphone over to campus minister and senior religion teacher Jeff Smay to lead us all in prayer.

"Good morning, seniors!" announced Smay, a thin, wiry man, wound tight with an enthusiasm that was too uncool for these kids. Determined, Smay chuckled, pushing his black-rimmed glasses back up his nose. "God is good!" he shouted, awaiting a response.

"All the time," murmured several of the crowd.

"Come on now," Smay encouraged them as he haltingly laughed. "You know how this goes!" Then again, with impossibly more enthusiasm, squaring both his feet in spirited determination, "God Is Good!"

The students sat up, following the lead of Chance, a leader on the football team, a cut-up around school, a genuine article, and, right then, the loudest person in the Great Hall. "ALL THE TIME!"

Smay nodded his appreciation that they were now joining in and then finished the cheer, "All the Time!"

"GOD IS GOOD!" The students were now looking around self-consciously at one another and laughing, maybe being just fine with this tradition as a beginning to their senior year.

I sat back in my chair. Now I was lost. For years I rode the history of who I was as a teacher at Fike High School, enjoying my reputation being handed down from older to younger siblings, from one friend to another, never considering that I would have to "introduce" myself to an entire school community again. As I pondered how to present myself, I witnessed the more seasoned faculty members here at Central comfortably take their turn in the spotlight, welcoming the students back with their own personal style which students had grown to cherish. History teacher Sally Beatty commanded the stage by leading the seniors in a "Maroon Knights" cheer then stoked their pride by shouting how "AWESOME" they were. Spanish teacher "Señora" Jan Grubler greeted them with a "Bu-e-nos Di-as!" slowly articulating each and every syllable, consonant, and vowel sound. All students, even those who did not take Spanish, repeated after her, earning a nod of approval and a nice, perfectly controlled smile from Señora.

The parade of teachers continued to dwindle down toward me, this new guy who became increasingly nervous about just how to present himself. I plowed through the list of items I had wanted to say while looking for some clue, some random thought that was flying throughout my scattered brain. "Relax," I thought. "Just be yourself."

♦

Fellow teacher Chrisola Ham and I stared each other down at center court for about two seconds before she started laughing. I wore my Superman t-shirt, jeans, and an intense attitude that told her I wanted to win this dance competition. My beady eyes darted around the gym while I loosened the muscles in my neck by bobbing my head back and forth. Students on both sides of the basketball court were cheering, laughing, or sitting quietly in disbelief as the music began to play through the loudspeakers in the gym. No one knew what was coming, not even Brandon.

We launched right into *Soulja Boy*, the more difficult of the two dances. Thank God we started with the harder one. I bounced from side-to-side with more energy than I should have had, using my peripheral vision to follow Brandon and the rest of the crew as they were crossing legs, stepping forward, swaying shoulders, and throwing punches. Sweat began to pour out the top of my head and rolled down into my eyes; I thought I was going to pass out from losing my breath. I was always a step or two behind everyone else, but, *damn, I was good!* I glanced over at Chrisola who knew the steps but could not stop laughing to let her swag shine, then I scanned around the gym to find the student body cheering and dancing themselves.

Now it was time for my showstopper as we segued into *The Stanky Leg*, a dance for which I only needed to watch Brandon so I could begin to get *my* groove on. Brandon was such a good teacher that I can remember the basic steps to *The Stanky Leg* even today. (Honestly though, all you do is simply lean to the right and gently push out from the opposite leg. Adding rhythm and style is another story entirely.) My showstopper involved putting my own touch on this dance so I raced over to grab a can from a plastic bag I hid near the bottom of the bleachers. As I swayed from right to left, I sprayed a can of lemon-scented air freshener all around the leg which I rhythmically extended as the "stanky leg." To finish, I tossed the can down, reached into the pockets of my jeans and removed handfuls of Starbursts which I gleefully tossed to my adulating fans as I swung my arms to the beat of the music.

Once the dance competition concluded, the student body gave us all a huge standing ovation. While Chrisola and I shared a big hug, she teased me, pointing out that I smelled through my sweaty Superman shirt, but that did not deter Brandon and the rest of the crew from coming over, animatedly congratulating me for my "off-the-chain" dancing then asking if I had any more Starbursts. I chuckled and thanked them for being such great teachers, setting off to find the nearest water fountain and air-conditioned room.

♦

I had stalled long enough, waiting for nearly all of the staff present to move towards Julie Shively to grasp the microphone for their turn. I am not sure why certain ideas manifest in my mind. I often wonder if I plant the seeds myself or some drunken magical Puck sprinkles glittering dust in my eyes to enchant, and at times, curse me.

Julie held out the microphone to me and smiled. "Go head, Mr. Bucon. Keep it short, OK?"

I bent my head down toward my shoes, wondering if my legs were shaking; then keeping my head lowered, I slowly raised my eyes to look at the senior class sitting out there, arms crossed, mouths clamped shut, looking back and forth at one another and then at me. I lifted my head, then cranked it around in circles in order to loosen my neck muscles. I looked at Julie and uneasily chuckled. "Sorry for this. You may want to step back."

I strode toward the students, twisting the microphone nonchalantly in my hand. I looked around for Emily, my tether to this new world I was entering. Taking a deep breath, I brought the microphone to my mouth, then locking my feet in a powerful Elvis Presley stance, I dove into an impromptu rehashing of "Heartbreak Hotel" delivered in a nervous yet earnest tribute to the aforementioned legend.

"Well, since my baaaaa-by left me," I sang into the microphone, "I found a new place to dwell." I pointed to my right then started a *Stanky Leg* twist on Elvis' infamous hip gyration. "It's down on the end of lonely street. It's C-E-N-T-R-A-L." Regardless of how clever I considered the change in lyrics, I was not feeling any love from the crowd, no cheering or clapping, not even a laugh, so I knew I needed to work a little bit harder to impress them as I curled my upper left lip to further find shelter in the King's shadow. "I been so LONELY, baby. Yeah, I been SOOOOO LOOOOOONELY, BABY! I think I could die!" I put my head down and thrust the microphone into the air.

Silence. Dead. Silence.

I looked at Emily who sat there with her mouth agape with a what-the-hell look on her face which ever-so-slowly transformed into a slight smile as I grinned apologetically and mouthed, "Sorry." I wondered what I could do to set this back on course, wishing that this was all some bizarre nightmare. I longed for a pocket of Starbursts.

I scanned the group of students, shrugged my shoulders as I returned from my out-of-body experience then made an incredibly abrupt change in tone and direction as I became a more dignified and controlled speaker. "Well, OK. That was weird. Thank you for being such a great audience. Now, if I could get someone to help me hand out a few papers." A quiet hush continued to hover across The Great Hall until Chance guffawed a solitary, deep-Italian whoop of a laugh, perhaps the only person in The Great Hall besides Jesus to catch the absurdity of what had just happened. The rest of the students followed with some quiet laughter, and a superhero rose from the small throng to save the day.

Earlier, as Jamie and I stood to the side and greeted the seniors who slowly entered The Great Hall for this kick-off meeting, she identified different students to me, attaching faces to names on class rolls of students. I always like to form my own opinion about their personalities so I took her insights at face value, realizing that tales of the past are not necessarily the narratives of the future.

People who know me can tell you of my affinity for all things superhero. From the time I was a child, I relished pouring through my comic books, reliving the amazing tales of Spider-Man, Fantastic Four, X-Men, and, of course, Superman. So, yeah, when someone wears a Superman shirt with a Superman backpack slung over his shoulders, I definitely recognize a kindred spirit. "That's J.T.," Jamie informed me when I muttered something about the Superman backpack being cool. "You are going to enjoy having him in class."

J.T., a somewhat short, blond-haired kid, wholeheartedly leapt through tall chairs and over round tables to help me distribute my papers to his fellow seniors. "I can help, Mr. Bucon," he smiled as he counted out papers for each table. His energy gave me a chance to take a deep breath and move past my personal perception of a disaster of an introduction.

I cautiously reverted back to traditional teacher mode, methodically skimming through my list of expectations for the first day of class, the books they needed and the materials which would lead them to success. I concluded my impression of a walking-talking bullet point list with an invitation to the group. "I am up in Room 301. If you have some time after this meeting to stop and formally introduce yourself, that would be great!" I blushed as I gradually retreated to my seat after that disaster, pretending to sort through my papers while wondering if I made the right decision by embarking on this impulsive, peculiar performance. Jamie smiled and laughed; I did the same.

One hour later I awaited visitors to Room 301, any seniors who wanted to take an early peek at the room Emily and I had established as our home for this year. I always entertain high hopes for a story to have a suitable ending; I possessed this skewed vision that many of these kids would bounce up the stairs with the same type of hidden enthusiasm that bubbled in my heart several days ago.

A quick rap on the door frame drew my attention from the organizing I had been undertaking at my desk. It was J.T. He entered the room, shook my hand, and introduced himself as he welcomed me to Central. He gave the room a careful once-over, checking out the student desk arrangements, the photo collage beside my desk, and, most keenly, the Marvel Comics Universe poster on the wall above the chalkboard. I could tell he was in a hurry as his friends were probably waiting for him to head to football practice. "Well, Mr. Bucon, I just wanted to come up and introduce myself."

"Thanks, J.T. And thank you for helping me out down in the cafeteria. I was a little worried about what I did down there," I admitted.

"Aww, no! It's all good!" J.T. assured me. "See you tomorrow!" He had another quick look around, smiled and nodded, then flew down the stairs.

We make connections every day of our lives: bumping into a stranger while exiting an elevator, speaking randomly to a person behind us in a checkout line at the grocery store, checking in for our appointment with the receptionist at the doctor's office. Other connections have the potential to be more long-lasting: greeting an inexperienced colleague where we work, welcoming an unfamiliar family to the neighborhood, introducing ourselves to new students or teachers. In most situations, we all desire to be seen in the best light possible. Unfortunately, true and rich connections take much longer to develop, much longer than a brief encounter.

I left the assembly that afternoon questioning what I had done and how I do things for reasons that make sense at the time but later grow to regret them. That is life for many of us. Hopefully we follow the instinct we possess in our hearts to be genuine, but there are times we are filled with doubt, an uncertainty that the image, the persona, the face that we offer to others is not going to be worthy, accepted, or understood.

Emily's mom Lisa texted me later that afternoon to ask how the senior meeting had gone. I responded that it was "OK," not acknowledging what to me had been a disaster. Lisa explained that Emily had told her about my singing with my first thought as she did so being "Oh. Lord." Lisa texted that the kids really liked it and were excited about having me as their senior year English teacher. Doubt still dwelt in the back of my mind even though some relief began to make its way into my consciousness.

In an effort to make these worthwhile, rich connections, we should put ourselves forward to others, transparently allowing a view into our singular character and soul. Sometimes we make an unpretentious moment a totally unnecessary production; sometimes we simply offer a helping hand to those in need. The truest test of the quality of our connections is when we make the effort from the heart, when we allow ourselves to drop our guard, when we exist in our discomfort, when we embrace our quirky or more subdued natures, and when we eventually laugh at ourselves. We will know when we have made a connection when people come knocking at our doors or when we walk to knock upon theirs.

5

The Metamorphosis

"So, do you all choose the prayer, or do I do it?"

My first class slid their *Day By Day* prayer books onto the desks in front of them, awaiting my announcement of the page number. "You do it," mumbled Nick, a stocky, somewhat intimidating football player who sat directly in front of me in the U-shaped desk formation Emily and I had set up for class. Nick begrudgingly dropped the book in front of him and waited. Emily, Chance, J.T., Nick, and the rest of the class all waited. I could feel their gazes, not aggressive, not oppositional, but more conciliatory, almost lead-footed while preparing for a daily prayer.

I spun my own *Day By Day* book atop the wooded podium on which I leaned, glancing out of the corner of my eye back to my daily objectives, the ordered list of every single task I wanted to accomplish each class period written neatly on the green chalkboard behind me. "The prayer. I forgot the prayer," I thought as I lowered my eyes back to the prayer book, an identical Notre Dame *Day By Day* book to the one I lugged with my school books when I was a student. A shiny blue, plastic-coated cover had evolved from the greenish gray cardboard-like cover from decades past. The prayers though, they remained the same. It was I who seemed to be out of sync with the world in which I stood.

The students waited, showing no enthusiasm, exhibiting no eagerness, and expressing no desire to pray yet again after having done so just the previous period. I felt I needed to hurry, so I quickly opened the book, intending to read the first prayer I found: page 79 - "For Good Attitudes Toward Sex." I snickered to myself, remembering how years ago I always wanted my teachers to lead us in prayer with *this one*. Now was my opportunity to be scandalous, now as a student who had awoken within a teacher's body. "Well, let's see," I nervously began then cautiously yielding to my better instincts for once, "not this one, but maybe we could…uh…" I quickly began to flip the pages in hope that I could find a suitable prayer among the Stations of the Cross, psalms, and the *Glory Be*.

"Mr. Bucon," J.T. interrupted to offer assistance. "We can just do 'Day By Day' on page 14. We all know that one." Everyone robotically opened the book to that page, again stoically awaiting me to lead them, to begin with the first words of the prayer.

Enthusiasm travelled hand and hand with me that morning as I arrived early, my companion as I sprung up the three flights of stairs, as I adjusted my tie each time I journeyed to the teacher's bathroom to relieve my anxious spleen, and as I greeted each student at my door before each class. Surreal. Three months earlier I had been saying goodbye to students at Fike High School for the last time and watched as they darted out of the school in their shorts, jeans, and t-shirts, celebrating that the unbearably long school year had finally ended. Three months removed, I now stood here observing the slow stroll of uniformed students - girls in gray skirts and white tops, guys in gray poly-blend pants and polo CC shirts – hardly enacting a funeral dirge on the first day of class at Central Catholic High School but quietly embracing a subdued enthusiasm at the start of the new school year.

In a transitory period which would later seem miniscule while contemplating all of the changes in my life, I still could not escape the anxious trepidation that I might not have my footing, that I had hit the ground running but not learned the lay of the land, the means to reorient myself to my new yet familiar surroundings. As always, I would take stock of my environment, draw from what I know and what I feel, then do the best I can to lead from the heart.

"Well, OK then. Let's do this." I made the sign of the cross as the students followed along, themselves preparing to launch into the traditional "Day By Day" prayer J.T. had suggested, but then I stopped them short with my own words.

"Heavenly Father, thank you so much for bringing us all together here today. Many of us know people from the past while others are becoming acquainted for the first time. Help us to have a good first day, a good senior year. Help us to keep in our hearts any personal intentions as we go through our day. And finally, help us to have a really great class. Amen." There was silence as we all made the sign of the cross and put away our prayer books. I would have a designated prayer from the book the next day, but I would always want to start each class expressing gratitude for having an opportunity to be where we are and to be thankful for the blessings we have in our lives. Somewhere along the line

I had learned that a prayer can only take a person so far if his or her heart is not invested.

♦

"Set up your seating chart. Discuss the syllabus on your first day. Explain all of your classroom rules and procedures." For the past twenty years principals, assistant principals, mentor teachers, and blind ritual have drilled these "first day procedures" into my head, into every teacher's head, as if there is nothing better than the tried and true way to welcome enthusiastic students into the class where they will spend the next semester or year. "Spend that first day establishing the tone and atmosphere of your classroom."

I can remember taping index cards to the upper right hand corner of every desk in the numerous classrooms I have called home over my first decade or so of teaching. Each index card contained a list of each period with one student's name neatly printed directly beside his or her corresponding period number. I always found it a joyful and empowering experience as a teacher watching my new charges scramble about the room to find their designated seats.

Experience eventually gave way to a relaxed wisdom. I tossed out those index cards and wrote a note on the chalkboard or smartboard which read: *Sit Wherever You Will Be The Most Successful.* Many students gravitated toward their friends, others opted for a corner in the far reaches of the room, and some even landed near the warmth of my burning presence of knowledge. My challenge to know about my students supplanted my need for organization and structure. Part of this came from a desire for a classroom which resonated a confident comfort, one in which students could be secure in the environment while being free to have ownership of their experiences.

In my formative teaching years, I used to wrap my syllabus and class policies talk all together on that first day. In an effort to trudge through all of the items, I would call on individual students to read aloud each item while I marked them present, writing their names on a perfunctory seating chart that kept them grouped as much as possible. This was an interminable routine for me, a day on which I wanted to do something original and creative with the students. When afternoon classes arrived, the students had typically experienced the same dull routine countless times. Who would visit someone's home expecting a list of routines and rules about each and every aspect of their visit there? Sure, they are not the same, the classroom and the home, but then again, I have found each moment in life to be one which is precious and invaluable, never to be regained once it is lost. As a teacher do I make this first impression with new students one which will be forgotten as soon as the bell rings or do I create one which sends them out the door talking, excited about returning the next day?

◆

"Alrighty then," I announced as we finished our prayer, not saying the actual "Day By Day" prayer while still keeping the spirit of the moment intact. I gave an unsuspecting Nick a stack of my syllabus and class policy handouts. "How about doing me a favor by passing these out, Nick." As he distributed the papers around the room, students began to glance over everything; being seniors, they had seen all of this countless times so there was clearly nothing new here for them.

"I am going to set this timer for one minute," I announced while pulling out a white digital kitchen timer then holding the second button down for sixty rapid-fire beeps. "We are not going to read every single item on here out loud, but I am going to point out the highlights of everything. Buckle up." I hit the start button then launched into a calm yet direct overview of the school rules, my basic discipline policy of "respecting everyone and yourself," the curriculum focus for each semester, and finally the supplies they needed for the year. With their undivided attention, I finished before the timer expired. "Please carefully read that entire paper front and back tonight, sign it, and write down any questions you want to ask me tomorrow. Now on to far more interesting things." Wide-eyes, smiles, and quick exhalations abounded as the students stuffed the papers into their folders.

I can recall times in my life decades ago, moments in a young person's life when I hugged a nearby wall for fear of embarrassing myself, out of dread of being ridiculed by shadows which lurked around me. These shadows never existed yet bellowed internal thoughts of rejection, the longing of a voice which yearned to talk, to sing, to philosophize, to create, to paint, and to write. Life has always been a quest to find a measured pace through times of jubilation and depression, up pinnacles of achievement, and out of the empty wells of failure. This journey permeates my pedagogy as an English teacher, as a sage of life, as a caretaker of knowledge gained in my short time here on Earth.

As an English teacher, I have opened windows into the lives of many novelists, playwrights, poets, and storytellers, countless auteurs who not only have a voice to be heard but a message either to be heeded or rejected by society. Through these windows my students have hopefully discovered stories, thoughts, and ideals which mirror their own. These windows are magical entry points for my students to discover their own voices and afford them an opportunity to understand this world much more than they had previously, but, if not that, at least this window possibly allows them to traverse and even come to appreciate the corner of the world which is theirs.

"You need to find one of these within the next three weeks." I lifted a maroon scrapbook off a nearby table at the front of the room, processing steadily and slowly, carrying it eye level about the room as if it were a sacred Catholic relic from a forgotten Holy Day of Obligation ritual. I learned long ago that physical objects can be entities of materialism and distraction while also serving as personal talismans, figurative drums, parchment, and canvases for those who need an instrument to tell their story or simply survive their lives. "The scrapbook needs to be eleven by eleven inches." I picked up a package of multicolored paper and held it beside the scrapbook. "You will also need your own cardstock paper so that you can personalize your pages."

I stopped. The enthusiasm that permeated the dusty classroom air just minutes earlier had now transformed into a consensus of bewilderment. The guys who lined the back rows with Chance and J.T. sat upright in their desks, a new tension removing any slouch in evidence earlier. They side-eyed each other with expressions of confusion and disbelief. Their quiet guttural scoffs led me away from them to the girls rustling uncomfortably near my niece Emily who sat there with an identical distressed expression she had after my Elvis impersonation a day earlier at the senior assembly. Nearby a petite girl named Shannon, a student who would rarely speak throughout the upcoming year, a student who would come to class every day prepared and would work diligently, looked at me with wide eyes and mouth agape long enough that the corners of her lips seemed to chap from the dry air. I needed to persevere despite their apparent confusion.

When a person has a vision that asks others to willingly follow, this person needs to paint a picture of the destination. I recall those Sunday afternoons when my dad would take us all on the dreaded Sunday drive. We never knew where we were going, how long we would be in the car, or what whims of my father would accelerate or decelerate the gas pedal. The randomness of the drive was so frustrating to me. The unknown destination required a trust that never quite developed in me as a child. So as a teacher I always place high value on making sure my students know where I am taking them. More often than not I successfully convey that message, but there have been times when the destination became lost amid detours that life had set in our path.

I opened the scrapbook to the first page, ready to show them where we as a class, where we as a group of individuals who were about to open windows to look at the world, where we as thoughtful and passionate people could experience an honest reflection of who we were in the past, of who we are now, and of who we could potentially be. "The first page will be the alphabiography." I continued to stroll about the room showing my students the page I had already created about myself. Colorful block letters of my name covered the page, all inscribed with a written passage concerning an aspect of my personality that related to each letter of my name. Layered beneath the letters were pictures of myself from various times in my life. Once I finished a general explanation regarding what we would do to create the alphabiography, I asked Shannon to pick a letter. She looked around, laughed uncomfortably, then asked for "B."

So I began reading that letter's contents to my audience, sharing with them an aspect of my life, establishing the idea that I will be asking them to "dig deep" into parts of themselves. "B," I began while clearing my throat, adjusting my posture, then cracking my neck for dramatic effect. *"Books have been open throughout all the pages of my life.* – See how the first letter begins with the letter of my name? – *Books have been open throughout all the pages of my life. I remember when I was a little kid, riding in our family's station wagon across the country. My dad would always yell at me, screaming to 'get my nose out of that damn book.'* – Oh, I probably shouldn't have said that word in front of you, but that is what he said. You can handle it. – *Sorry, Dad, I kept on reading and am now telling my students to 'keep their noses in their damn books.'"* The class laughed quietly at that then asked me to read another one.

Once I had read each passage corresponding to each letter of my name, I turned to my résumé, the page after the alphabiography, noting that the first two pages are about presenting two sides of yourself, the creative, personal one and the professional aspect of who you are, to anyone who would be reading the scrapbook. Nods in affirmation began to percolate throughout the class as my students became not only more familiar with this year-long project we were undertaking but also more familiar with me as a teacher, much more a person, who would be guiding them throughout the year.

The final page I showed them that first day was a creative interpretation of Franz Kafka's *The Metamorphosis*. "OK, so on this page here I am dressed up as a bug." I had made the page years earlier when the idea of the scrapbook monster first raised its ominous head back in North Carolina. I had my friend Susie take pictures of me dressed up as Gregor Samsa, the main character of the book, as he emerges one morning as a bug. I had dressed in all black: black pants, black jacket, black toboggan, black sunglasses, imitating Samsa as he slowly exited a room, crawled across the floor, and sniffed a picture of Susie. Of course, no one gave two cents about what I had written about the page or the book. They fell over one another in a hilarious struggle to view the pictures of their English teacher dressed like a bug crawling over the floor.

"A bug?!?" Chance would laugh, clearly calling me out for ridicule in front of everyone. "You dressed up like a bug?" Everyone awaited my response to Chance's ribbing.

"Well, yeah. What's the big deal?" I chuckled and shrugged. "I thought it was kind of cool." The bell rang, sending my new students out of our room babbling about a scrapbook and laughing about "bugs." I smiled as I watched them leave, yelling out the door behind them, "Thanks for a great first day! See you tomorrow!"

Six years later at a Central playoff football game in which Chance was now an assistant coach for the team on which he once played, I would bump into a group of these same students, many now graduates of West Virginia University. We would talk about that first class of ours together, the scrapbook which many of them still treasure, the end of the year commencement presentation, and whether or not the students are still doing all of these class activities. One of the gang even teased me, asking me if I had dressed up like "a bug" lately. We would all marvel and laugh at the crazy stuff we all remember.

We began a metamorphosis of sorts that year. After spending two decades as a teacher five hundred miles away in North Carolina, I had reemerged at my alma mater where I had walked the halls some thirty years earlier. I was now ready for the next stage in my evolutionary process. These students, the CCHS Class of 2013, Emily's class, my first class, were along for the ride, taking a journey with a crazy man who had once dressed as a bug. On that day all of us jumped in my car, I pushed down hard on that gas pedal, and we accelerated into the future while having only an inkling of the possible destination. On that day change was just fine since we all appeared ready and anticipated the ride.

6

Taco in a Bag

I stood uneasily on the sweltering sidelines near the CCHS end zone at Wheeling Island Stadium, a gangly Central freshman anxiously awaiting my premiere as a multi-talented member of the Maroon Knight Marching Band. The mammoth bass drum protruded from my chest, dangling and swaying from the hard grey holster which shed particles of foam as it pressed down upon my sweaty t-shirt. I struggled to tighten my back in a useless effort to find a comfortable standing position as the clock stopped and restarted while the football game lurched to halftime. Looking like nine-month pregnant women on the back row of our drum corps, two other bass drummers and I stood waiting for that buzzer to signal us to the field where we would march to our school cadence in as much unison as a group of teenagers could muster on this searing August evening.

A.J. Bucon

Once the clock expired, we waddled our way to the end zone, lining up in preparation to divide the football field in half as we marched toward *The Barge*. Mr. Tony Shoto, our beloved band director, blew two long whistle bursts followed by three short tweets as we stood at attention in our positions beneath the field goal bars. *Hweeee! Hweeee! Hweet! Hweet! Hweet!* We all tapped our drumsticks on the rims of the bass and snare drums; the cymbal carriers smashed a quick muffled clash on the fourth beat. *Click. Click. Click. Hwoooosh. Click. Click. Click. Hwoooosh.* The pomerettes shook their maroon and white pom-poms as we proudly began our rhythmic drumming, the cadence we all knew, loved, and hated, the one which still marches through my memory from time to time numerous decades later.

Dum! Dum! - Dum! Ditty! Dum! Dum! - Dum! Ditty! Dum! Dum! - Dum! Ditty! Dum! Dum! – Dum! Dum! Dum!

This was my moment, our moment. Being in the band was huge for me because it proved to be my vehicle for traveling from one end of the angst-ridden teenage spectrum to the other. I was sweating, wearing thick maroon polyester band pants rimmed on the cuff with white shoe polish from sporty chalky band shoes. We were all pounding on our drums, clashing our symbols, or jiggling those pom-poms in an effort to awaken those disinterested people in the home stands, to hold them in their seats until the end of our show before releasing them to the musty restrooms and concession stands. No one but our parents, their friends, and a bunch of random folk really gave much of a damn actually, and that was just fine. We marched forward - *Dum! Ditty! Dum! Dum! – Dum! Dum! Dum!-* until we reached *The Barge*.

My Corner of the World

♦

I left Wheeling, West Virginia, for Wilson, North Carolina, back in 1991, less than a decade from when I graduated from CCHS, so *understatement* is the best word to characterize my observation that it had been a while since I last saw a CCHS football game on Wheeling Island. Earlier that week as we were finishing up a vocabulary quiz, J.T., Nick, and Chance asked if I were "going to the game" Friday night. Those three and many of their friends were senior leaders that year on the football team, a team who year after year had one goal in mind, to play in the West Virginia State Championship during the Super Six Weekend on Wheeling Island.

"Going to the game" has been part of my vocabulary for numerous years, rooting itself in innumerable contexts. As a student and member of the band, we boarded a packed band bus as we were "going to the game" where we would play the fight song and victory march to support the team, then take the field to entertain the fans. As a teacher for nearly thirty years, I always made plans for "going to the game" where I hoped to see my students in their element, but as I grew older, I seemed to never have enough time or energy to attend as many events as I would have liked. As an assistant coach, head coach, academic adviser, braintrust member, side-kick stat man, or part time water-boy over ten years at Ralph L. Fike High School, "going to the game" involved more than just collecting basketballs and volleyballs, washing smelly uniforms, and counting heads on a darkened bus; it was a lifestyle which opened my eyes to the flip side of the high school classroom, another avenue of instruction and role-modeling. As a parent and uncle, "going to the game" meant a return to the stands, this time as a personal cheerleader, someone to be there as family for my son Robert, Emily, and, of course, my nephew Chris. The back of my door is full of ball caps that I have worn to games. Some caps are tattered while others are much more crisp and new; all are comfortable for whatever the context happens to be.

That first game I sat near the top of the stadium with my brother Jim, his wife Lisa, and their friends. The crowd of humanity adorned in shades of maroon, gray, and white buzzed incessantly throughout the huge Central faithful with fans sporting *The 2012 Football "Band of Brothers" Shirt*, family members attired in oversized football jerseys with their last name embroidered on the back, everyone wearing articles of clothing which exhibited their spirit and pride. Mini-kingdoms of families and friends spread across the slanting landscape, staked out invisible yet open borders with long blankets or towels across the bleachers where everyone camped together, with queen mothers clanging cowbells for every outstanding play.

Scanning the crowd from our particular kingdom, I easily captured the landscape of this world, one which is like so many other communities across the country, one in which everyone appears to have a place, a small portion of the larger backdrop. Two familiar figures slowly extricated themselves from the student section near the bottom of the stands where seniors occupied the front rows, leading the cheers, insisting that the obnoxious and silly freshmen stand for the team as it warmed up on the field rather than sitting in the back giggling and laughing like the grade school urchins they were a year ago.

My Corner of the World

"Hey, Lisa. Emily and her friend are coming," I quietly announced. The pair of friends made their way through the stands, stopping to laugh and talk along the way. I gasped when my old folk vision came into focus as the two moved closer and closer to where we were perched near the top half of the stadium.

Emily and her friend arrived, wearing clothing designated as the theme for the game: maroon and white. Back in the day, decades ago, wearing maroon and white for a game typically meant a t-shirt and some touches of face paint. Of course, we had the Maroon Goons who designed war-paint masks of maroon with touches of white smeared across the entirety of their faces which transformed them from ordinary high school students into rabid maniacs who joined with others to form a mob of spirited insanity which seemed just as significant as the game itself. People claim that times change, and, in fact, times do have an ebb and flow. Still, school spirit typically remains consistent. Emily and her friend wore maroon shorts with cut-up t-shirts whose sleeves were missing as a result of a clear case of scissors gone wild in what must have been a hilarious moment of unfashionable fashion design. Rounding out the humorous outfit were tube socks pulled completely up to the girls' knee caps with maroon and white ribbons tying up tufts of hair atop their laughing heads. I relished being here in this current scene and was able to appreciate it in the context of school-spirited escapades I have both experienced and witnessed in my life.

Lisa talked with both of the girls, smiling and asking about their lively outfits. My brother Jim sat up behind me, not wanting to venture into that conversation and choosing to stay focused on the game about to begin. I smiled and told Emily that they looked really nice as I noticed the maroon and white handprints friends had randomly placed all over the exposed skin of their bodies. What a colorful mess they were! The Maroon Goons would surely be impressed by the new newfound use for maroon and white paint.

As the pregame clock crept closer to zero, Emily smiled, looked down at the student section, and announced their goodbyes. In varying degrees of enthusiasm our little kingdom encouraged them to have fun as the girls raced quickly down the stadium steps in all of their maroon and white enthusiastic glory.

♦

The cadence ended with a *"Dum! Ditty! Dum! Dum! – Dum! Dum! Dum!"* I exhaled, dropped to my polyester maroon right knee, placing the weight of the bass drum on the grass of the football field and unhooked the clasp joining me to my huge percussion instrument. Fellow band members did the same as we situated the drum sticks and mallets atop the percussion instruments and disconnected the harnesses. We pulled our drenched white t-shirts away from our clammy skin to allow the warm air to cool us while we proudly jogged to *The Barge*.

The Barge sat there near the edge of the football field, pulled to the center by Mr. Brinkmeier's pick-up truck. I am sure *The Barge* derived its name from the actual barges which floated coal up and down the Ohio River back in the seventies. This was not a barge though. It reminded me of a float from a big Christmas Day parade somewhere, a float which had been stripped of all its ornaments and designs then painted white. Maybe it was an old hay wagon which had been refurbished and painted, iron bars added which jutted to the sky for a maroon canvas canopy to cover the musicians who played on board during the football halftime. *The Barge*. That is just what it was called. Where it came from, who thought of it, which band boosters put it all together was of no consequence to us at the time. *The Barge* was our stage for this moment in our lives.

We tiptoed around the confines of our portable stage, careful to avoid knocking a clarinet, flute, or saxophone off the metal folding chairs lining the front row. Those of us in the back row, the brass section, the trumpets and trombones, maneuvered ourselves into a position that would allow us the elbow room and arm space the woodwinds in the front row did not need in their comfortable chairs. The pomerettes separated themselves into smaller groups on each side of this moving platform of musicians and stood ready to present their routines with our music as accompaniment. Our cramped environment on *The Barge* juxtaposed on one hundred yards of wide-open football field seemed as humorous then as it would be now.

Honestly, I can barely remember all the songs we played that season. I can remember Robin with a bowler hat atop her head dancing with a cane to our version of the Nitty Gritty Dirt Band's "Mr. Bojangles." Later in the show we would switch to a classic version of "Disco Inferno" from the soundtrack of *Saturday Night Fever* as Lisa and Michelle would spin and toss blazing fire batons to the sound of "burn, baby, burn – disco inferno." Other songs found their way into the set, but the CCHS victory song (actually the Notre Dame Victory March with the lyrics slightly changed) always ended our halftime show. We did not march off the field after the fight song but simply climbed down from *The Barge* with our musical instruments in tow and moved past the water buckets steaming from the extinguished fire batons. We formed lines ahead of the actual percussionists who simply clicked-clacked their drumsticks and mallets in unison allowing us to fall in step as the band left the entertainment spectacle that was *The Barge* for Mr. Brinkmeier to pull off the football field before the team returned.

We band members returned to our personal spot in the stadium adjacent to the student body with only an exit ramp to separate the two groups. A chatter about the show rattled throughout our entire section with talk of how well the show went, who was out of step, or who noticed the fire baton that would not stay lit. The content never mattered much in the long run, ultimately becoming forgotten gibberish in our memories. The show was about us, our work, our talent, and our contribution to the community.

The third quarter was our opportunity to take a break, so we all scattered in different directions. Some of the juniors and seniors sprinted down to the restroom where they could sneak a quick smoke in a locked bathroom stall. The concession stand offered other people a chance to grab a paper cup of pre-poured Pepsi which had grown watery from the ice which had melted since being added at the end of the second quarter. Still, the Pepsi was perfectly fine to wash down a warmed-over square of DiCarlo's pizza wrapped in tin foil, a stale, table-salted bag of popcorn, or a boiled hot dog on a soggy bun. More often than not, I chose the latter, but I had to go check in with Mom and Dad first to grab spending money. With that cold cash came the obligatory congratulations on a good show and nods of affirmation for a job well done from everyone in my parents' own little kingdom. Eventually I would need to leave so I could return by the end of the third quarter, just in time to play the fight song one more time.

◆

I stood in front of the Wheeling Island concession stand menu sorting through all the items available while people anxious to return before the end of the third quarter waited impatiently before moving to the next available line. The square pieces of warmed over DiCarlo's pizza had been replaced with a slice of Domino's pizza pulled from a modern pizza warmer; my white stale popcorn had popped into freshly made yellow popcorn with kettle corn available at a table across the way; and the plain boiled hot dogs with mustard and reconstituted onions were now available with cheese or chili sauce. Toss in nachos and cheese with or without peppers, big hot pretzels, Gatorade, bottled pop, water, and a mix-mash of candy like Air Heads and Blow-Pops, and I had abundant choices only a person with ADD could appreciate. However, I came for none of these concession confections I had already enjoyed in my travels to many football stadiums, basketball gyms, and baseball diamonds here and in North Carolina. I came for something new.

After halftime I saw several people eating a peculiar item in the stands. They dug hard into orange-red bags, pulling out a mixed forkful of broken orange chips, chopped pieces of lettuce and tomato, beef, cheese, and sour cream. I have an eagle eye for food, a bloodhound's nose for possible quarry; I zeroed in then nudged Lisa. "What – is – that?" Licking my upper lip while impolitely pointing like a small child who knows no better, I turned back to those people who were eating and laughing.

Lisa leaned over and laughed. "Oh, God. That's Taco in a Bag."

"It looks so good." I know she saw my eyes glazing over.

Lisa shrugged her shoulders and shook her head, "I don't eat that stuff, A.J.," but she knew of my affinity for stadium food. "You need to try it though."

I stood at the concession stand, considering the best possible combination of food and drink. I looked at the CCHS Booster parent who stood behind the counter. "I will have a bottle of Pepsi (screw the caffeine) and a Taco. In. A. Bag." I said it slowly and clearly so that she would not get the order wrong.

"Do you want everything in it?" she asked.

I was stunned. I squinted my eyes in enthusiastic confusion.

She laughed, "You know, lettuce, tomato, taco meat, cheese, sour cream. Everything."

I looked from the counter person to the prep lady patiently waiting at the Taco in a Bag station for my response. I smiled, cocked my head, and finally answered, "Sure. Everything, please." I stood back and watched the lady clad in a maroon shirt and white apron make my order. She opened the large snack bag of Doritos, releasing the protective nitrogen, then proceeded to apply a firm yet gentle crunch to the chips inside the bag. Moving to a slow cooker, she scooped out what I would later discover to be a lovingly generous spoonful of taco meat and gently poured it into the bag of broken Doritos. She sidestepped with my bag down to the table's prep section where she sprinkled the lettuce pieces, tomato bits, and the shredded cheddar cheese into the bag, eventually topping the concoction with a glorious dollop of sour cream. She inserted the fork directly into the bag then commenced the procession from the back of the concession area to present me with my first Taco in a Bag.

I was tempted to eat it right then and there, but I decided to return to my seat in the stadium where I could continue to watch the game. I carefully closed the top of the Doritos bag, picked up my bottle of Pepsi, and wound my way through the slowly dispersing crowd.

I situated myself a few rows down from where I had been sitting with Jim and Lisa. I opened the bag and peered inside to what appeared to be a bit of a mess, a mixture of veggies, meat, cheese, and smashed Doritos. It did not look appetizing. I started to think about Grandpap and how he used to mix everything together on his plate whenever we ate dinner at his house where he would always shrug and laugh, claiming "it all goes to the same place." I took my fork and began to chop, jab, and mix the contents of the bag into a work of art that only I would ever see or taste.

I ate forkful after forkful of my Taco in a Bag, savoring each mouthful as I relaxed, comfortably immersed in this time and place. I watched my new students on the field as they won their first game of the year. I watched as all of the various kingdoms in the stands stood and applauded, clanking those cow bells. I watched as the student body cheered in their maroon and white garb, celebrating a new year, a new chance for endless possibilities. I watched as the stadium quieted while the team, cheerleaders, and coaches met at the fifty-yard line for a post-game talk and prayer. I closed my eyes after taking another more deliberate mouthful, thinking of what this world was like for me as a teenager who, like so many others, struggled to find reassurance that this was his world, too. I opened my eyes to see my past, present, and future blending together into one community, much like my Taco in a Bag. I was once and still remained a member of this community in which all could have their own niche, their own sense of belonging, and their own kingdom high atop the bleachers. I swallowed the bits of taco which remained, washing most of it all down with a cold gulp of Pepsi. I opened the Dorito bag one last time, digging the fork into the corners for any Taco in a Bag that remained.

7

The Scrapfolio

When the movers unloaded the huge truck here in West Virginia, I did a workmanlike job unpacking boxes of household items and clothes. The earlier boxes were more compact, neatly organized, and labelled with the contents. The more recently packed boxes, the ones which were last in the sorting and repackaging of my life in North Carolina, the ones into which I shoved the endless remaining items that did not have specific categories or necessitated immediate opening, became either treasure troves of rediscovered joy or cardboard boxes of the misplaced and lost. Regardless of where I placed the plaques, pictures, books, and figurines, time would need to serve as my assistant in making sense of how all these representations of places I have been and people I have known fit together. I found no way to create a picture of my past other than closing my eyes and digging deep into memories as I handled each item I unpacked and unwrapped from newspaper or bubble wrap.

In the rear of the laundry room I found three cardboard boxes marked "SCHOOL STUFF" in an extra-thick black Sharpie. I had already opened one several months ago, scrambling for files, pens, knick-knacks, and books to carry to school when Emily and I were setting up my classroom. The others had remained unopened, packed tightly with those random items for which only I would know their intended purpose, a magician's suitcase of tricks to entertain or inspire audiences, some magic we all need in our lives, that intangible essence to create wonders in our world.

With the enthusiasm of a young child on Christmas morning and the care of an archeologist inspecting his greatest discovery, I judiciously examined each item, scrutinizing its function in my future plans. I smiled as I placed colored card-stock paper overflowing a plastic grocery bag apart from everything else as the beginning contribution to my "need this" pile. Child protective scissors, the ones with the dull edges, blunted points, and small finger holes were also added to my "need this" pile. Rubber-banded rolls of motivational pencils enclosed in an old metal Bazooka-Joe bubble gum container started the "not yet" pile. Elmer's glue sticks, used once or twice, so much more effective and less messy than glue bottles, joined the "need this" pile with a mental note: "Need more. Need many more." Boxes of paper clips, boxes of staples, and boxes of thumbtacks were quickly moved to the "not yet" pile. Then, finally, I discovered the item for which I searched, the one which was integral to my project, the one which lights up, the one which cuts, the one which can create jagged edges and curves with its fancy, interchangeable attachments. My handy-dandy paper cutting board. My "need this" pile was complete.

♦

My Corner of the World

When I arrived at Central back in mid-July to pick up insurance papers and fill out payroll forms, Julie Shively presented me with a canvas bag of textbooks: The Prentice Hall Series: *Timeless Voices, Timeless Themes*; The Norton Reader, 7th edition; Immaculée Ilibagiza's *Left to Tell*; and Sadlier's Common Core *Vocabulary Workbooks, Levels D, F, and G*. Over my twenty-plus years of teaching, I have perused and selected numerous sets of books, adopting updated versions which were aligned to new state-standards that changed every five years or so, comfortably and uncomfortably changing lesson plans to utilize the materials which were now at my disposal. As a new teacher, one who was fresh out of college and the student–teaching experience, I appreciated the invisible companion of a Prentice Hall editor, a spirit guide found in a portable box of teaching materials which graciously accompanied each class set of textbooks that the county or state chose to adopt. They were aligned to the new collection of standards so all I needed to do was follow the book, print the premade quizzes, reading guides, and tests, then subsequently grade all student responses with the readily available answer keys. My teaching life was going to be so grand back then!

As I became more and more experienced as a teacher, I slowly discovered that these are simply tools, two by fours, or building bricks, not the be all and end all of a classroom or learning environment I would want my students to ever believe is the foundation of inquiry and education. I grew disenchanted, not with the selections within the adopted and mandated texts (well, maybe some of them) but with this idea that all students think alike, achieve alike, fail alike. As a teacher I have introduced and taught students selections like James Hurst's "The

Scarlet Ibis" or Maya Angelou's "New Directions," reading with my students in class and asking them to finish the selection on their own then to complete the prescribed questions at the end. I could easily dig through the teaching supply box or workbooks for a premade worksheet on symbolism or imagery, print it, then ask the students to simply complete it under my guidance, normally filling in the blank boxes with responses which would ring as eerily similar to one another. A teacher can fall into a trap here, particularly if that is the end of the learning process. I am a proponent of students taking steps past this point to create something of their own, an extension of what has been learned or examined.

I am no stranger to standardized testing. I have journeyed there with my students hand-in-hand, brain-to-brain, through tedious test preparation which can be an obnoxious mind-numbing process for students and teachers alike, particularly if the tests are "high stakes" (which means that a course grade, grade level shift, or college placement will be the ultimate reward for achievement or undesired cost for failure). I support accountability in education, but I struggle with tests being the *only means* of assessment, particularly standardized tests given during a three-hour frame of time. This was one of the sad reasons I chose to leave North Carolina as the testing was beginning to occur in every subject, at every grade level, with a never-ending expectation of growth each year despite having different students who had different academic challenges and unique social factors outside of the classroom. Teaching and learning had become so much more to me.

My Corner of the World

So the first weeks for my new students at CCHS was different from what they might have expected from me. I do not think Nick, Emily, and the gang expected to dive into the summer reading that no one bothered to read, Immaculée Ilibagiza's *Left to Tell*, an incredible true story told by a young Tutsi woman who was the age of Emily and her friends when a horrific event befell the author. During the Rwandan Holocaust of 1994 Immaculée loses the lives of her Tutsi family and is forced to hide in a tiny bathroom with seven other women for three months in order to escape the Hutu tribe's bloody slaughter. When I stumbled upon the book in the canvas bag Julie Shively had given me in July, I immediately read it, finding Ilibagiza's account of this tragedy so incredibly personal and shocking, its relevancy nearly lost on a summer reading to Emily's class. It remains a story to be heard by current generations, a book about faith, loss, and forgiveness. So we dug deep, we took our time, we made the book ours. We began with basic inquiry: What are the characteristics of a holocaust? Where is Rwanda? Who are the Hutus and Tutsis? Why is there conflict between them? How many people were executed? What role did countries around the world play in this? What role did the United States play? How was the Catholic Church involved? Without context, the story is certainly one worthy to be read; with context, the context which Emily's class discovered and shared, the book is a remarkable treasure, one which allowed the students in class to see beyond our protected world in Wheeling, West Virginia, into a world on another continent, a beautiful world turned brutally violent.

In my classroom at Fike High School I had a framed quotation mounted in the back of the room and would always point it out to students who were in a teenager's rush to finish an assignment. It read: "Wisely and slow, they stumble that run fast." Friar Lawrence warns Romeo in William Shakespeare's classic tragedy that sometimes it is best to be smart and take our time with important matters. If we do not, we tend to make mistakes, falling into bad situations in our haste. When we rush, we all miss being present in moments which could inevitably be of greater value for us than if we sped through them. We slowed down, we read *Left to Tell* in smaller pieces, completed journals about what we had read, and found quotes and passages that were not only inspirational in Immaculée Ilibagiza's precarious situation but also relevant to our own lives. We had our seminars in the u-shaped format as we listened to one another and our own perception of what life would have been like for us had we been in the author's situation. There were no handouts or charts to fill; there was just the book, a journal, and our own voices.

While my students immersed themselves in *Left to Tell*, I spent my free time scouting for a special place in the school away from the classroom where we could set up camp for the special week-long activity I had been planning. I happened upon the old school library, dusty and quiet, a collection of six nicely sized wooden tables set together near the opposite end of the rows of bookcases. Religious statues stood on side tables and the check-out counter: the Infant of Prague, the Blessed Mother, Jesus with his nail-marked right hand raised in peace. The metal blinds allowed for enough ambient light to enter the room throughout the day to create a feeling of dawn constantly arising. This would be our place. I took a big piece of cardboard and some markers then created a welcome sign made up of intentionally uneven, unbalanced, colorful

My Corner of the World

letters that I would place on the door at the outset of Homecoming Week: Senior Scrapbook Day!

♦

Signs for Homecoming Week occupied all open spaces on walls throughout the school, reminding everyone from the mighty seniors to the lowly freshmen what to wear for the week instead of the gray, maroon, and white uniforms. Monday was Favorite Team Day, Tuesday was Twin Day, Wednesday was Generations Day, Thursday was Mass Day (please dress in uniform for the Lord), and Friday was Maroon and White Spirit Day. Homecoming Week had been planned for months; the dress up days were only part of the pageantry which included honoring the Homecoming Court, a rosary rally at the Cathedral, a parade down National Road, the Friday night game on Wheeling Island, and the Homecoming Dance Saturday night at Oglebay Park. I have always secured everything in my classroom, put my head down, and just plowed forward with a smile on my spirited face until life returns to normal.

My own enthusiastically made sign was taped to the board in the classroom where everyone could read it as they entered the room. Homecoming Week would also include the soon to be yearly tradition of Scrapbook Week, a time to stop the vocabulary lessons, halt the journal writing, and put aside ongoing textual analysis essays. I wrote my bulleted list of materials on the green chalkboard adjacent to the sign:

- ✓ Bring scrapbooks!
- ✓ Bring mounting paper!
- ✓ Bring pictures!
- ✓ Bring any art supplies you need!
- ✓ Bring a good attitude!

While there was not the shock and confusion of *The Metamorphosis* bug reveal, the class was a mixture of eye-rolls and skepticism along with a hushed enthusiasm.

"So that's all we're doing next week?" questioned Chance, the designated voice of the football players who were going to be preoccupied with thoughts of the big game on Friday night of Homecoming Week.

"Yep. That's it. I just want you to spend the time enjoying the opportunity to be creative with your class," I told him and the rest of the curious listeners. "It will be fun!" I never should have added that prediction. Students, even adults, myself included, can become queasy when informed that the unknown will "be fun."

♦

As I stood in the library, the bell rang for my first class on Monday of Homecoming Week. I have been teaching for over twenty years, yet I still become anticipation's willing prisoner on days when I present something new to my students, an activity that I simply know will have long-lasting effects despite any initial trepidation in their minds.

Chance entered the library with Nick beside him, both looking skeptically around for where they should sit with their scrapbooks which were hidden at the bottom of a stack of books carried at their sides. Emily and J.T. followed behind, both of them carrying their bags of supplies with a welcome sense of happiness, one not overly exuberant but one which let me know they were ready for this. The rest of the class slowly made their way to the tables as the seconds ticked away during the three minute class change. I grabbed my phone and popped outside the door to catch the stragglers. I found John, my student I called "Johnny Mac," and Shannon looking at the sign I had transferred to the outside of the library door. "Hey, you two," I playfully barked, encouraging them to move to each side of the sign. "How about a picture in front of the sign for Scrapbook Week?"

Johnny Mac was always cool about stuff and told Shannon where to stand. He threw up his hand in front of the sign and asked, "How's this?" Both laughed and smiled for my impromptu photo shoot then proceeded inside to join the rest of the class.

The tardy bell rang and I started with our traditional prayer, zipping through it in an effort to start right away. "I am going to do this quickly now. God will understand. In the name of the Father, and of the Son, and of the Holy Spirit." Everyone followed my lead. "Heavenly Father, thank you so much for giving us the opportunity to come together again today. Please bless our Scrapbook Week. Help us to find inspiration in our efforts, to be patient with ourselves and others, and allow us a chance to have some fun while doing this." We all made the sign of the cross then dove into creating our scrapbooks. Well, sort of.

Earlier that morning before the students began to arrive at school, I had placed plastic baskets on each table, baskets filled with glue sticks, safety scissors, markers, and crayons. On a separate table my own scrapbook lay open for the group to see so they could perhaps find some inspiration in my pages. Beside my scrapbook was the lighted craft board. Once we finished the prayer, I pointed out all of the materials, demonstrated the cutting board, and waited for them to begin. There were a few people who embraced the spirit of the day and began by throwing open their individual scrapbooks, cutting card stock paper into letters for their alphabiographies, and transcribing their written descriptions of themselves onto index cards. Nevertheless, the majority sat there, hands clasped together, not with a pretense of defiance about the activity but simply unsure, having reached an impasse in regards to doing something creative and personally reflective.

From the beginning of the year, Emily's class was typically "all in" regarding whatever we were doing, but as with all journeys, the path can be fraught with insecurities and doubts. My experience with students and creativity is that many young people behave as we adults often do. We compare ourselves, who we are, what we chose to create, and how we reach our vision to other people who are simply attempting to accomplish the same. So we set about that week creating our alphabiographies and our book pages with an attitude about the process of becoming. We were learning to be OK with what we did, learning to be OK with handwriting that was not as neat as someone else's, learning to be OK with an odd color combination or a sheet of card-stock cut not quite as evenly as we would have liked, learning to be OK being in awe of an artistic friend's cleverly layered design without being threatened. By the end of the week we were all letting our guards down a little, allowing our ears to be open to advice, permitting others to lend us a hand, learning more about one another in a creative, spirited community.

As Friday arrived, we were afforded a moment of reflection as the class sat around different tables. Students moved from group to group to see the final products of the week and mingled with peers with whom they did not typically associate. I sat down at different tables to listen to their comments to one another, to hear the laughter about how bad some pages seemed to look when compared to others, and to witness the pride of having completed a project that many did not think possible at the outset of the week. Johnny Mac was one of those who struggled with the whole creative aspect, perhaps providing an indication why he was last to class on Monday. "Mr. Bucon, where did you come up with all of this stuff? I mean, did you just wake up one day and decide to do it?"

This scrapbook activity had caught many of the students unaware. They were certainly not ready to accept the assignment at the beginning but became more curious as we completed it. Johnny Mac's question was a good one. He forced me to personally put some pieces and experiences together and to consider how I had reached this moment. So I dropped my guard and took my audience of students back nearly eight years earlier to North Carolina.

My nephew Chris graduated from Central the year before Emily became a freshmen. I had made plans to fly back to West Virginia from North Carolina for his graduation, but I struggled with finding just the right graduation present for Chris. Yeah, I gave him a card and some cash, but that does not say "I love you" like a truly thoughtful gift. What could I do though? I had moved to North Carolina a year or so before Chris was born and spent much of my "uncle time" five hundred miles down south. As I did with Emily, Chris and I spoke on the phone, checked out his mom's pictures on social media, and spent time together whenever I came home over Christmas and during the summer. I have always been a photo person; my family typically runs whenever I want to take a picture but is always grateful later when I share a great moment. So as my nephew Chris' graduation approached, I began to look through old photo albums where I found an idea for the perfect present.

 I gave Chris his graduation gift as soon as I arrived in Wheeling the day before his graduation from Central. He carefully unwrapped the box to discover his personalized Uncle AJ Scrapbook and began pouring through the pages which proceeded chronologically through the life of Chris as I had seen it—not just pictures, stickers, and decorations but something much more. Each page was a window into a memory I had of Chris as he was growing and contained a handwritten reflection on that time period in his life and what it meant to me, his uncle. The previous month had been a journey in itself, printing and ordering pictures, slicing card-stock paper with my lighted craft cutting board, writing, revising, and then transcribing what I wanted to say to my nephew. Chris pored through the visual manifestation of my thoughts and memories. He laughed at the Oglebay Good Zoo page on which he found pictures of his toddler self and me gliding down the roller slides at the zoo and his posing in front of the otters which playfully swam behind the glass where Chris rested his hand in hopes of touching one. Chris shook his head at the page dedicated to his love of the Thunderbirds, Wheeling's minor league hockey team. There was Chris, a young goalie wearing a hockey uniform, protecting the hockey goal his mother and father erected in the backyard for him. Once he finished, Chris picked up the scrapbook and laid it atop all of the other plaques and pictures that would be on display at his graduation party the next day, informing his mom that the scrapbook needed to be front and center.

A year later the scrapbook idea made its way into my International Baccalaureate English class at Fike High School. After all, I had the cool lighted cutting board, leftover glue sticks, a crazy idea, and some unsuspecting students. We embarked on a unique journey together, reading Kafka's *The Metamorphosis*, Voltaire's *Candide*, and Esquivel's *Like Water for Chocolate*. We wrote analysis essays about them, we conducted seminars, and we made some wild scrapbook pages: a creative *Metamorphosis* page, a *Candide* comic strip page, a *Like Water for Chocolate* family recipe page. I remember at the end of the semester, students had to complete IB-mandated individual oral presentations about a topic of their choosing from any of the selections we had studied. I remember Beth and Elena suggesting that we just do an oral scrapbook presentation. This idea led to our huddling up in a circle for the week while each student took turns discussing one of the books, using the scrapbook pages as a basis for their thoughtful presentations, going through the author pages, the social and cultural context pages, and finally their unique creations about the novel on which they focused. This was the last time I did the scrapbook idea in my classroom in North Carolina as a year later I had boxed all of the leftover glues sticks, the remaining card stock paper, the child protective scissors, and, of course, the lighted cutting board and moved back to Wheeling, West Virginia, and Central Catholic High School.

"So that's it, guys," I concluded. "That's how this whole scrapbook idea came into my head."

Looking past the four pages he had completed and onto the empty pages that remained, J.T. asked if we were going to do all that my students in North Carolina did.

"Oh, yeah," I told him. "That and so much more." They had no idea. None.

Shannon's eyes popped open again as they did when I first told them about the scrapbook months ago, her mouth launching into a smile as she held tight to her scrapbook. The entire class did something similar with some smiling as well, others nonchalantly rolling their eyes, while a few just took to staring at me with no expression whatsoever.

Mason was one of those students who could always find the back row in any classroom, not to hide necessarily but to remain at a comfortable distance for observation and independence. Sometimes Mason would offer an irritating remark or cynical comment to make light of what we were doing; so when he started mumbling and laughing to himself, I sighed and prepared myself for the worst. "You know, Bucon," Mason began as he flipped through the alphabiography page, the résumé page, and the *Left to Tell* page. "This really isn't a scrapbook. I mean, it *is* literally a scrapbook, but you tell us it is going to have more papers like our résumé in it, too?" He laughed as he annoyingly flipped back and forth from page to page. "I mean, we *are* writing on every page so this is more of a writing portfolio."

"What are you saying, Mason?" I took a deep breath, always hypersensitive to criticism and worried where Mason was going with his observation.

He looked from Chance to J.T. then to Emily before finally blurting, "It is more of a port-book or something."

J.T. chuckled and ribbed Mason, perhaps in an effort to take the attention off me and my possible reaction. "That is so stupid, Mason. That doesn't make any sense. A *port-book*?"

Mason rolled his eyes while everyone laughed at this idea, not realizing that he had inadvertently uttered the inspiration that would change the way future students would refer to this project.

"Now, wait-a-minute, everyone," I announced, pushing through my own reaction to this hilarious idea. "Mason, maybe you have the right idea but just have it backwards. You know, port-book does sound strange."

"So what then?" Mason asked. "How about scrapfolio?"

The laughter throughout the class completely reversed itself from a tone of ridicule to a tone of positive affirmation for Mason's idea. And that is where it started, where the windows to their worlds would open, where their past experiences would intersect with their present lives, sparking voices of who they are in their own corners of the world. "That sounds fantastic, Mason. Scrapfolio it is."

8
Standards of Doubt

Two full days of my life were gone, frittered away in a blurred struggle to focus during the drudgery of a two-day staff development. Months away from my phone call from the principal at Central Catholic High School offering the opportunity to return to my alma mater, I was in the middle of North Carolina's first push towards aligning everything to the newly established National Common Core Standards.

North Carolina was among the first group of states to be awarded a *Race to the Top* federal grant, a rather hefty monetary support to encourage these states to be trail-blazers in the adoption of the Common Core Standards. As with most grants, there were strings attached: the mandatory staff development, the realigned curriculum to meet the standards, the shift in teaching methods, and, of course, the sharing of test data. I can barely retrace my bog-hopping steps through numerous learning initiatives among the local boards, state legislatures, and federal government. Before President Barack Obama's Common Core implementation, educational communities directed efforts towards addressing President George W. Bush's *No Child Left Behind* initiative, creating, as we did in North Carolina, programs like the *ABC's of Public Education* as educational leaders saw the writing on the wall years ahead of time. We had a lengthy timeline which implemented testing schedules, Student Accountability Standards, and Adequate Yearly Progress formulas to measure the growth of students throughout all subject areas. While I understood and still believe that accountability in education is important, NCLB and Common Core became invisible monstrosities whose tentacles rooted themselves in all aspects of the school environment through an overreliance on test data as the final word on student achievement. Educators alike knew there was so much more to what transpired in a classroom than what could be identified in test data.

The two days were excruciating as a mixture of administrators and teachers who had trained to develop and present this staff development swirled through premade handouts, played instructional videos, moved through slide after Power Point slide, and led activity after collaborative activity. Their audience? Teachers. Regardless of how benevolent the presenters are or how much candy they offer in supplication, teachers are the absolute worst audience *ever*, particularly when unknown individuals tend to "teachsplain" to a group of experienced educators the manner in which content should be taught in our classrooms, the expectations teachers and local educational collectives should have for achievement, or the types of assessments those same groups should use to evaluate their students.

I remember doing my best to be a dutiful participant, but, to be honest, I reverted to my base instincts once I had the gist of the standards, finding all of the videos and handouts overkill for standards which are basically common sense. Hiding my cell phone in my lap, I texted Felissa, Kim, and Kathy, fellow English teachers who were assigned to opposite tables, then waited impatiently for them to check their phones and smile. I slipped through a stack of student essays I needed to grade but found they gave me headaches. I noted that I wanted to download that Lionel Richie country CD *Tuskegee* because one of the Letchworth twins continued testifying about how good it was while forcing those of us at our table to listen to it during much needed breaks. I was falling completely off the downside of any attention span scale, but at least I remained somewhat quiet and stayed within the confines of the small fortress erected at my table. Other teachers around the room continued an incessant questioning of the presenters about the Common Core, some defiantly claiming it was a liberal agenda to ruin education while others struggled with the idea of measuring accountability. Hands of exasperation were flying in the air before, during, and after the breaks which made the entire atmosphere one of chaos and confusion for many of us. Those poor presenters! If they were wise, they would have stashed a bottle of whiskey in a back room for quick shots during each break. Thank God I was not in their place. Not in a million years.

◆

One Friday afternoon my junior honors students were busy in their groups helping one another understand the different features and personalities of the characters found in Geoffrey Chaucer's "General Prologue" from *The Canterbury Tales* when Becky Sancomb, assistant principal at CCHS, walked into the room. She floated around the classroom, stopping by each group and its messy amoeba of desks to have a closer look at what the animated students were doing. The "General Prologue" has always been a challenging piece of literature to explore, particularly since it contains no plot or narrative and establishes the premise for the tales themselves. I have always found the prologue unique because it offers a written microcosm of society during The Middle Ages, a portrait of the colorful group of pilgrims who were beginning a journey to the shrine of Saint Thomas a Beckett in Canterbury. I rolled out my silly take on *The X-Files* television show called *The Canterbury Files* to my juniors; it was a multi-faceted project meant to engage them on many different levels, demanding multiple modes of thoughtful expression, collaboration, and creativity.

Becky is always insightful when observing what students are doing in the classroom and perceives the ultimate purpose of any activity, so as she made her way from group to group, I eavesdropped during my assistance and observations elsewhere. Students showed her *The Canterbury Files* overview I gave them, a document which broke down the overall project into various challenges, steps, and due dates which culminated in a final presentation. Becky examined several dialectical journals which contained excerpts regarding each of the pilgrims in *The Canterbury Tales* their group were to examine. Multiple lines of Chaucer's text were mirrored by each student's own thoughts, interpretations, and questions in these black and white composition journals. As with typical high school students, there were the random demonstrative sighs of overwork and impatience in the project itself, but Becky ignored the lame and whispered cries for help by smiling and advising them to continue working hard.

My Corner of the World

When the bell rang, Becky remained until the students left in order to talk with me. "This is a cool idea," she began. "Are you really going to be able to do all of those things in that project?"

I laughed, giving her my smart-ass "you doubt me?" look, one which she would eventually grow to love and hate over the years we spent together at Central. "Um, yeah. I think so, but it may take a while."

"Let me know when you present the final product. I want to see those," Becky said, always there to bear witness to my class's final products semester after semester and year after year.

"Without a doubt. Now, it may be a week or so." I paused to look through some of the work the students had already completed then quickly changed my mind. "Make that two weeks."

Becky laughed then dove into the original reason she had wandered up to Room 301. "Julie wants you and me to get this Common Core unit plan going." She sighed with one of those fake, uncomfortable "I don't want to do this either" smiles, and I knew exactly why. We both knew the confusion and animosity of so many teachers regarding Common Core itself. The additional expectation of a detailed unit plan with little clear, relative direction was only serving to add proverbial fuel to the fire.

"Sure, Becky." We both chuckled. "We'll get together later." Becky left me to my students' folders, a mish-mash of desks scattered about the room, and my racing thoughts.

◆

I sat at my kitchen table on Oakdale Drive in Wilson with my dog Ranger sprawling on the floor beside me where he rested after his dinner. On the other end of the phone I held in my hand was Julie Shively, the newly-hired principal at CCHS, the retired Air Force officer I had met nearly a year ago in her school office during my summer trip to Wheeling. This was an informal meeting, hardly what I would have considered a job interview, but it still opened a door to the possibility of a return to Central. At that time, I was impressed with Julie's direct nature and long-term vision. Slowly reaching a level of burnout in my career in North Carolina, having grown frustrated with the daily ritual of trudging up and down the hallways at Fike High School, I was looking for a change. While the meeting remained in the back of my mind for most of the school year, it did afford me an opportunity to allow the idea of a major change in my life to simmer. Until now.

"So, Mr. Bucon, we would love to have you come to CCHS next year as a member of our English department," Julie informed me. "If you are interested, we can talk about some of the details of your contract."

We continued our conversation, discussing the salary, the unfortunate lack of real benefits, and the job requirements. I knew that moving from a public school teaching job to a parochial school position would mean the loss of some definite perks in a public school, but I had already weighed much of that and was blessed with a plan which would enable me to make the move without much of a disruption to my life. Yes, I was taking a cut in salary, but this was important to me. My son Robert was grown now, living on his own with his wife Emily and their son Justin. I was in a muddled funk at Fike where I felt stale and uncertain regarding what I wanted to do on the backside of my teaching career. My mom was growing older as well so the call to return to family and life in Wheeling had become louder than the one that I had always heard in the distance. Perhaps the time *was* now. Doubt did permeate my decision-making process, but gut-instinct took the reins for this part of the journey.

Our respective schools were in the second half of the year, slowly but surely making our way to the end of the year with an eye to the future. Julie and I talked about what both schools were doing when the topic of Common Core arose unexpectedly. She explained how the Diocese of Wheeling-Charleston was asking everyone to align to the standards but that many of the teachers at Central and around the Diocese were struggling with it. I offered my take on the standards, encapsulating the two-day workshop I had experienced a month earlier for her while conveniently omitting my own personal feelings of frustration and indifference. Maybe I should have been more honest about my experiences with implementing standards and testing before Julie took the opportunity to hopefully interject, "Mr. Bucon, you are going to be such a big help with the staff. Having that knowledge about Common Core will help so much as we continue to change how we educate our students."

I laughed, explaining to her that I could "help" but was not comfortable explaining Common Core standards to everyone. I did not want to become that person, one of those presenters from my two-day staff development when I had hoped they had a bottle of whiskey in the back room for themselves. I just wanted to go to Central to teach, to enjoy and reflect during the second half of my teaching career, to reorient myself to the comforts of a local community and culture I missed tremendously.

A.J. Bucon

♦

I emailed Becky to tell her that I had developed my own version of the unit plan the Diocese was asking teachers to create to demonstrate that we were aligning our lesson plans and instruction to meet the standards of Common Core. I had been uneasy when Becky visited me at the end of the previous week about creating this unit plan as there was so much prologue to her request.

Weeks after our first meeting in the Cathedral following our kick-off mass in the chapel in which corners were claimed and positions staked, Julie started the ball rolling on the creation of these mandatory unit plans. We had a Microsoft Word template to use as a basis for the unit plan that few, if any, could understand; we had a confusing set of expectations regarding the purpose, the creation, and any subsequent evaluation of completed plans; and we were a combustible mixture of teachers with varying years of experience, differing ages, and personal as well as political opinions on Common Core. There was no one-size-fits-all example, no model for each subject area, and no guide for each teaching style. The afternoon meetings about these unit plans became an externalized battle during which everyone became frustrated. My OCD control issues were fluctuating between resigned ambivalence and shoulder-tensing anxiety as these constant meetings dampened the joy I was experiencing in my classroom. I asked my questions, I listened to others, I explained my understanding of Common Core, but I had no desire to step into the fray to lead this effort. None whatsoever. I just wanted to focus on my senior *Left to Tell* discussions and junior *Canterbury Files* projects. I wanted the dysfunctional chaos of these unit plans to fade away and ultimately disappear. Unfortunately I felt as if I had time-travelled half a year in the past back to my two-day staff development in North Carolina, but this time the two days were endless weeks.

I *would* create a unit plan. I had done many plans like this in the past. I would make one which would be professional, one which would be specific, one which would be aligned to each and every goal, one in which I underlined specific words from the standards. I would eventually spend hours of my free time obsessing over the creation of a color-coded spreadsheet with nifty hyperlinks and feel proud of what I had accomplished, regardless of the fact that it was not something I would have chosen to do on my own.

Becky entered the computer lab next door to my room where my juniors continued working on the next phase of *The Canterbury Files*, Power Point presentations which featured slides of each one of the Canterbury pilgrims. She poked around as she normally did, looking over their shoulders to ask them what they were doing now. The juniors had their books and dialectical journals opened on their laps, transferring text onto each one of their individual slides, creatively adding pictures of what his or her respective pilgrim would have looked like then as well as what his or her counterpart would be in the here and now of the twenty-first century. The groups debated about color styles and slide layouts, accepting one person's idea and rejecting that same person's suggestion later in favor of another collaborator's proposal. The groups were so engaged in this stage of the project that they did not have time to eavesdrop on my and Becky's quick conversation.

"Here," I handed Becky my "Anglo-Saxon Unit Plan – Verbiage Underlined," a stunningly overwrought three-page spreadsheet chart of alignments, grade designations, course levels, a leading question, a Catholic component, Common Core standard numbers to the decimal point and beyond, detailed activities, an allocation of days, a taut list of resources, working hyperlinks to documents and videos, formative assessments, summative assessments, and a free download version if purchased on Blu-ray. It was orgasmic. Totally. It meant nothing, but it meant everything. I know my eyes were beading with excitement and anticipation for her reaction.

"Wow," Becky whispered as she read through it. "You've been busy. When did you do this?" The question was one that emanated amazement as well as concern for my well-being. Becky was only discovering my cursed blessing to obsess over the minutest detail of anything important to me and, for that matter, anything that had begun to fester under my skin.

"This weekend," I told her. "I fixed a pot of coffee and went to town." As God as my witness, that is exactly how I spent four hours on my Saturday morning toiling over a unit plan which in many ways meant nothing in the grand scheme of my life or the lives of my students. It had felt good though. Whether it was a logical, point by point explanation for how my students learned or an angry scream of overwhelming frustration at being asked to actually spend my free time laboring over this was of no consequence to me at this point. I did feel a genuine sense of accomplishment as I watched Becky continue to read the unit plan with the color-coded spreadsheet cells, the perfectly aligned objectives and standards, and the thoughtful insight into my teaching practices.

♦

Days later I stayed energetically riveted to the tasks at hand throughout my classes, overseeing the final Power Point slides and facilitating the drafts of the puppet show scripts for my juniors' *The Canterbury Files* project. We were all so close to the end of this project I had envisioned so long ago. The students and I finally moved to the same page as they began to assume more individual control over important decisions for their final products. The quickly approaching presentation days generated a renewed enthusiasm and sense of pride for what the students had accomplished.

At the end of that school day, I powered on my smart board, glanced at Jesus beside it, knelt before my computer to open my Dropbox file as I retrieved "Anglo-Saxon Unit Plan – Verbiage Underlined," then awaited my colleagues who had also just completed their own days with students. Julie had called a meeting so that I could present my unit plan to everyone as a possible example of how to complete their own plans. I had forgotten my whiskey bottle at home so I relied on the morning remnants of cold coffee settling in my mug and a half-empty bottle of water as I braced myself to become one of those presenters I had pitied six months earlier in North Carolina. An inner voice fostered doubt in my mind that countered any sense of pride about my unit plan. What was I doing? Why am I doing this? I had not even made it to Christmas here, and I had pushed myself into a quagmire of confusion, uncertainty, and frustration. I needed to hold back the anxiousness and simply keep at the forefront of my mind the idea that "I just want to help." If I am anything, I am fairly altruistic with a goal to make a situation a little better than when I arrived. On certain occasions like this one, I do experience misgivings about whether what I am actually doing helps the situation or makes matters worse.

I smiled half-apologetically as people entered the room. Jeff Smay walked in with his usual enthusiasm, paper and pen in hand, while others filed into the room with a dejected appearance, one that forcefully begged for release from this process. Jamie Campbell slid into a desk near the door close to the smartboard, smiling at me in an attempt to buoy my spirits. Jamey Conlin lumbered in, looking for a seat in the back so that he could witness the entire experience from a vantage point of discretionary distance. Julie and Becky walked in last, ready to begin this somewhat impromptu and tense staff development meeting.

"Good afternoon, everyone. Thanks for coming," Julie began then nodded at me. "A.J. has a finished unit plan that I want you to see. I am thinking we will use this or some form of it as our template for plan submission." She carefully surveyed the group to make sure everyone was present and ready to begin, then Julie finally tossed me a nod to start. "A.J.?"

As I looked out at my audience, I noticed everyone sitting with the same groups as they had when we met that first day in the Cathedral. We may have moved the location for this meeting from the earlier sacred confines of the Cathedral to a classroom where just an hour ago my students were drafting scripts for a puppet show, but the contextual setting remained the same. The seating was not theater-in-the-round for this meeting as I stood on the edge of the proscenium, no longer a passive observer in this play but an actor who seemed frozen in a spotlight of his own making. So I pulled back the curtain as I brought up the tab which featured the unit plan I had worked so hard to complete, the one for which I felt so proud, the one which I uncomfortably placed on display for all to peruse.

When once I had channeled some deranged spirit of Elvis as I introduced myself to the senior class at the beginning of school, I needed to step away from my discomfort and embrace what I needed to do and accept the reaction. This time a clever song would not work on my audience, so I put my proverbial head down and did what I came to do—explain my work, honestly, openly, and unapologetically.

I began at the top of the spreadsheet, worked my way across each color-coded row, then proceeded to the next, meticulously explaining my thought process. As I marched my way through my work, I would occasionally look out at my audience, an attentive one but one which beautifully masked its feelings. The scene in which I felt the centerpiece was a poorly constructed one, one in which an atmosphere of community effort had been splintered long before I addressed my first classroom activity on this chart, one which was not quite glued back together at the early Cathedral meeting. When I was done, Julie resumed her leadership role in all of this, responding to questions, some of which only served to stoke the embers of my own discomfort.

"So, you want us to do something like this?"

"Do we really need to be this detailed?"

"Who is going to read this?"

"Are we going to actually do this in this format?"
"What happens if we do not do it right?"
"Who is going to help us with this?"

My classroom had become a hub of confusion, animosity, fear, and curiosity, all mixed together, ratcheting up the stress levels surrounding these unit plans. Jamie Campbell tossed me an uncomfortable smile of support, nodding as she packed up her papers and headed back down to her room. Sac followed her, more tired than he seemed to be last summer, quietly looking down at the floor as he checked both directions in the hall while leaving my room to make sure he was not bowled over by oncoming traffic. A few stayed to continue talking to Julie, asking her pointed questions, digging deeper into her and the Diocese's expectations. I glanced at Jamey Conlin who smiled in the back row while talking with Sally Beatty. Eventually the entire staff left, some offering appreciation for my efforts and others offering nothing more than a impersonal view of the side of their heads as they drifted back to their rooms.

♦

My unit plan presentation grew heavier on my shoulders as people's questions and comments fell into my daily routine. My colleagues sought me out for assistance on the unit plan, many genuinely attempting to do one of their own, with others actively deriding the entire process while passively noting what I had done with my unit plan in comparison to theirs. I offered my help as best I could. This is all I ever wanted to do. Unfortunately I felt as if I had become the de-facto authority of Common Core I never wished to become. By no coincidence several students began to ask me directly if what we were doing in class was "Common Core," concerned that I was exposing them to some terrible disease. "Please stop." I would ask them. "Do not get caught up in labelling something. These are going to be great presentations!" I had to persevere through any doubt that I was experiencing to remain focused on the ultimate goals for my classroom, goals which simply had not found their origins in any personal effort to align with Common Core or in the creation of a unit plan I was required to make.

I smiled at the detractors and proceeded with my classroom projects. The juniors continued their work on personal paper bag puppets of the Canterbury pilgrims. Our room became littered with scraps of construction paper, pieces of felt, and random strands of yarn. The juniors started noisily practicing with their puppets, finding their own unique voices as they rehearsed the stories they had in their scripts of the pilgrims growing to understand one another on their journey together to Canterbury. The Knight spoke commandingly with his son, the Squire, about how to follow the traditions of knighthood while elsewhere the Pardoner had quite the humorous conversation with the animated Wife of Bath and the Miller. I set out to create a stage for the upcoming presentations by breaking down an old box I had unpacked from North Carolina, then taping on "Go, Knights!!!" signs I had discovered in a closet on the second floor of the school. We were all enthusiastically pressing forward in this now seemingly endless project as the end finally appeared in our sight.

Jamey Conlin would catch me on my way out near his first floor classroom one day. "Bucon!" he yelled from behind his computer screen where he was busy inputting quiz grades amid paper-clipped stacks of student work. "You got a minute?"

"Sure. What's up?" I asked walking into his overly organized room where learning objectives were written neatly in chalk across the blackboard near his desk adjacent the door. They were posted in a place where there would be no excuse for students not seeing them as they entered or departed the room. If I did not know better, Jamey probably took a ruler and measured the space between the objectives. They were so damn neat, so perfectly spaced. The desks had all been returned to straight and orderly rows; not one pencil, paper, or book seemed to be out of place. To say that Jamey was a god of organization was to do this math teacher a disservice, one which he would laugh off with embarrassment.

Jamey swung a rolling office chair around for me to use and asked me to sit down. "I just want to pick your brain about some things." My spider-sense tingled. After all, the days since my unit plan reveal had been filled with so many different attitudes, personalities, insinuations, and questions that I was just tired, beat down, and ill-prepared for any more thoughts or questions about what was in my plan or how I taught. I know Jamey saw exhaustion on my face, so he began slowly. "First, how is it going? How are you doing, A.J.?"

Those were an odd couple of questions. I would eventually learn that Jamey always genuinely wanted to know how everyone—students, colleagues, and friends—was doing. It was a question people could expect from Jamey in the best of times and the worst of times. "I am fine, Jamey. Just a little tired of things right now."

"You mean those unit plans?" he chuckled.

I laughed, "Yeah, those and other things." I was purposely vague, not being in a state of trust with many people at that moment. I shared some inconsequential tidbits but held my true feelings close to my chest.

"Yeah, I know what you mean. Let me ask you something. I am just curious. You were teaching in North Carolina for a long time, and you have been here for a while. Do you see any noticeable differences between where our students are academically with the students that you taught there?" He sat back in his chair with a look of curiosity for my response.

Given the climate of the first half of the year, this sounded like an offer to take sides in some battle of which I still had no desire to be a part. I wanted to be direct yet as clear and objective as possible. "Jamey, I have found that young people are young people wherever you go. The kids here are great. Are they where I think they need to be academically compared to the ones I taught in North Carolina? Honestly, I cannot really make that comparison in fairness to both groups."

Jamey wanted more, "Yeah, I know that." I think Jamey struggled with the question he asked and the answer I gave as much as I did.

"Look, are there things I wish my students already knew?" I began. "Sure, but that is my job to take them there. I cannot change any experiences that these students have had here or at any other school before I arrived. I need to meet them where they are. I can only make sure I am doing my best to prepare them for their futures based on where they are now. But the answer is 'no,' Jamey. I do not see a big difference.

There are students who struggle and some who excel. I am not sure if that answers your question."

Jamey nodded. "It does." While I am not confident about how much it did answer the question or even the context of the original question, Jamey and I felt comfortable enough to drop any pretense in order to sit and talk some more about both of our experiences in education. It was a good afternoon, one in which I started to feel a bit more comfortable as a new teacher here at Central. In the future Jamey and I would continue to have even more philosophical discussions about education, students, life, and even death.

On my way out, Jamey stood, shook my hand, and then stopped me one more time before I left. "Bucon, one last question."

"Damn, Conlin. Another?" I laughed. "What?"

"That unit plan. Seriously. I don't want to offend you," he half-laughed, "but how much time did it take you to do that?" He finally burst out his big Conlin laugh. I knew instantly the context of that question and what he was implying by asking it. We were both teachers, ones who understood the qualities of a successful classroom and how any time taken away from nurturing that was time not well spent.

I rolled my eyes and shook my head dejectedly. "Entirely too damn long."

We both laughed together as I left the room. "Later, Bucon!" he hollered down the hall as I made my way to the parking lot, feeling a little bit better about how I was going to move forward.

♦

My Corner of the World

The juniors and I had pushed the desks back against the side walls as much as we could for the first *Canterbury Files* presentation. Becky made her way back to the room for the culminating presentations. The groups who were not delivering theirs sat anxiously awaiting the show to start. This project which began weeks ago actually developed a bizarre life of its own, evolving into a monstrosity that I never expected. That is part of the magic that can happen in a classroom when students become invested. As a teacher I had set the project in motion, but the students took it where they envisioned it could go.

The first group began by introducing themselves and the name of their group. We all listened to each student discuss the character he or she had been assigned as the group delivered its Power Point presentation. Yes, it was uncomfortable for many of the students as few enjoyed talking in front of people, but the presentations clicked as the peers in the group stood side by side in support of one another. Once the Power Point presentation ended, the group erected my make-shift puppet show stage atop a table in the front of the room, slid their hands inside their paper bag puppets, and began to prepare for the show. The remainder of the class insisted upon pushing the desks back even farther so they could all sit on the floor in front of the puppet show stage. I asked them why in the world they were doing that. They explained that when they were young, they would sit on the floor in front of the stage when they watched puppet shows. The lively puppet shows were full of laughs and shenanigans as the students took their impressions of these characters who lived during the 14th century and portrayed how they could have possibly related to one another on their journey to

Canterbury. All of these told a joyous story, not just of the pilgrims, but of the students who toiled together throughout the duration of this project.

Those Common Core unit plans continued for several more years, always remaining a source of contention for most people but gradually becoming commonplace and inconsequential, needing that occasional email from Becky to remind us all of the due dates. As for myself, I became less concerned with the process of writing one and more cognizant of the time and energy I invested in its creation. I desired more time to create new *"Canterbury Files"* projects for my students, ones which allowed them to engage a topic whether it be a piece of literature, a speech, a play, or a video, ones which encouraged them to interpret and knowledgeably understand ideas for themselves and then create extensions of these thoughts in the forms of analysis essays, blog posts, artwork, videos, and even puppet shows.

To this day, doubt always follows me around. It can be a shadow on my brightest of days, one which questions, sometimes kindly and sometimes extremely critically, the decisions I make in my classroom and in life. Doubt is the shadow to my burning desire to move past preconceived notions of myself or of my abilities. I have grown to accept that I will always have doubt as a companion to my aspiration to create a better world than what I see around me. I accept both doubt and desire together as part of the experience of life and as a testimony that I may actually be on the best path for myself as I travel down an unfamiliar road—much like the pilgrims on the road to Canterbury.

9

In the Palms of Our Hands

The root cellar in our home in Bellovedere is situated under the stairs adjacent to the large garage beneath the house. The chill of the basement and the root cellar in the center of the house made the perfect locale for Mom's storage of self-canned items like green beans, beets, pickles, tomatoes, and peaches. Eventually, as the years passed and our garden disappeared, the shelves which held the garden harvest slowly became shelves of empty and unused glass canning jars interspersed among a hodge-podge of vases and sanitized plastic JIF peanut butter jars, the latter which Mom would refill a couple times a year with her homemade strawberry jam.

Mom would sort through the root cellar in the basement when I was young. Store-bought canned food became the norm as we all grew older, but Mom still kept this entire cellar in order, noting how many kidney beans, tomato sauces, or peas we had, counting the number of paper towels or dish soap bottles. I developed Mom's regular habit of taking stock of what I had in order to make sure I always had the bare necessities for the future.

When I lived in North Carolina, Mom would tell me about the CCHS canned food drive. Lou Volpe, my senior English teacher when I was a student at Central, was instrumental in the development of this service project decades ago, conducting it during the month that led up to Christmas. The food drive has become a yearly tradition at Central, one which continues to make a vital contribution to the shelves of "18th Street Center," the more familiar, around the town name of Catholic Charities Neighborhood Center on 18th Street in East Wheeling.

By the time I had arrived at Central, Lou Volpe had retired, leaving the framework of the entire project to those who would carry the project into the future. Jamie Campbell had assumed the reins of this project, fashioning it into her own vision. The local Kroger and Riesbeck's grocery stores donated swatches of large brown grocery bags. The senior government classes spent days stapling fliers which explained the drive, the types of items 18th Street Center would accept, and the pickup dates to each of the thousands of bags, moving each completed stack to the pews of the chapel where the students could retrieve them the day of the drive. The regular schedule of classes moved to the back burner as this day became one dedicated to the entire service project. Students dressed in their Maroon Knight hoodies, jeans, and solid walking shoes as they filed onto buses which would carry them to different parts of the Wheeling area.

My first year I took my sophomore homeroom to wind our way through the streets and neighborhood near Saint Michael Parish.

Trusting them to break into small groups, I gave them maps of the area we were asked to canvas, then I sent them on their way to traipse up and down the streets of the neighborhood. They placed the brown paper bags on the inside of screen doors or under welcome mats with the hope that in a few weeks Central students could return on an early Saturday morning to find the bags full of cans or other food products which parents and Central community volunteers would transport to 18th Street Center for sorting and distribution to the needy families in Wheeling.

◆

My mom and her friend Chris had been working at Catholic Charities' Neighborhood Center for many years. Mom began to volunteer sometime after I had moved to North Carolina and found a unique collection of people with whom she would spend her time volunteering in the community, making this locale a vital element of her life, a journey which no longer had my brother or me anywhere close to being underfoot.

Every Monday afternoon dinner shift at 18th Street Center became Mom's three o'clock destination where she would prepare the Jell-O salad or chopped fruit for the lunch delivery the next day. Once this labor-of-love was finished, she and Chris would assist in the food preparation for the dinner crowd. This was Mom's special time, one during which she worked side by side with Chris, Sally, Chet, Sister Constance, and Sister Teresa. They were her group, a caring band of people who supported Mom which allowed her to remain purposeful in her life while nurturing her soul with the joy of serving the less fortunate.

Anytime I came back for a visit from North Carolina, whether it was the Christmas holiday or summer vacation, I went with Mom to 18th Street every Monday. During long distance phone calls between West Virginia and North Carolina, Mom often regaled me of her experiences working there over the years, lovingly extending an implied offer for me between the lines of her weekly tales to join her and her friends every Monday. These days were a way for me to share in Mom's world from afar, to be part of the good that the center contributed to this area of Wheeling.

Sister Constance and Sister Teresa are two dear souls who continue to play a significant part in Mom's life. Both of them are beautiful people who see the good in others and speak so kindly and affectionately in their melodious Irish accents. Sister Constance, a thin, devout woman people respected tremendously for her hard work and dedication to the poor, was in charge of 18th Street Center when Mom first began volunteering. Years after Sister Constance retired, Sister Teresa, a short and enthusiastic bespectacled angel, became another source of spiritual guidance for Mom. One or the other always greeted both of us over the years when we would visit. Sally was their kitchen manager, one who empathized with the lives of the people who would walk through the doors of the center because she had battled many of the same issues they encountered. Sally ran the kitchen for Sister Constance and Sister Teresa and would always have some preplanned task for me when I arrived, whether it was peeling and slicing potatoes and carrots, moving boxes from one floor to another, or sorting through the clothes or supplies in the back room. These were jobs that I would graciously embrace as I would help 18th Street Center run smoothly, jobs that I would see as part of a much larger picture once I returned to teach at Central.

◆

Thanksgiving was just around the corner, and we had recently completed all of the work on *Left to Tell*, finishing up with a viewing of *Hotel Rwanda*. Engaging the content of both had been depressing for many despite the optimism of the central characters. Reflecting on the violent loss of family members that Immaculée Ilibagiza experienced during the Rwandan Holocaust and her ability to forgive those who perpetrated these horrific crimes encouraged many of us, myself and students alike, to jettison any small or major transgressions we had experienced in our own lives. In that way, we could once again appreciate life with a greater awareness of the power hate and anger can have in our lives. The true story of Paul Rusesabagina, a hotel manager who hid over a thousand Rwandans during the massacre, saving all of their lives with this personally dangerous choice, also brought a focus to the compassion and assistance we can provide to people who live in dire situations.

This class experience served as an opportunity to reflect on the meaning of gratitude. How would we feel if we were to lose the people in our lives to a violent massacre? How are arguments about homework or chores actually inconsequential when we realize the blessings that we have around us? How often do we take for granted the sacrifices of parents, grandparents, other family members, teachers, coaches, and even strangers have made in our lives? How often have we expressed gratitude for those who have carried us when we are at our weakest? These questions carried over into my senior class as I thought I needed to turn the corner towards something creative, to shift into a more upbeat tone. The holiday was forthcoming so why not leave for Thanksgiving break taking stock of that for which we felt grateful?

Ann Kahle, a laidback seventies child, claimed her art classroom down the hall from mine as her world. As my years at CCHS would progress, I would find myself in Ann's room asking about types of paint, ways to cut and shape paper, and advice on art projects. Ann was one of the teachers who had taken a genuine interest in the creative aspects of the scrapfolio, such as the alphabiography and the book pages. We definitely found common ground as I would use art as a vehicle for students creating their own voices. My students would always travel back and forth between our two rooms looking for Sharpies, glue sticks, or colored pencils.

I had this quirky idea about how I wanted to create the next page in the scrapfolio. The project would be messy and original yet somewhat nostalgic in its basis. "So, Ann. If we paint our hands in class, what type of paint do we use?" I held up my hands to examine my own palms before holding one up to Ann. "This can't be hard, right?"

Ann's eyes would widen quickly then close as she started to laugh at my naïve outlook on this actually being easy to do. "Well, what are they going to do with their painted hands?"

"I want to have a handprint there on the paper. I kind of thought that after we paint our hands we would smash them down on card-stock paper. The paint won't bleed through that, right?" I laughed then proceeded with the project details, taking Ann through each step as she listened to what I envisioned as the final product. I knew it had the possibility of going wrong in so many ways as visions of paint splattered across the tables and floors with large flecks flying on school uniforms, but I was determined to give it a try.

We talked for a while as Ann offered suggestions that would make the project much easier to manage, some red tempura and sponge brushes, and finally her art room sink for washing and cleaning purposes. Before I left, Ann helped me to make my own handprint, a definite requirement since I always wanted to do whatever my students were going to do, even if it involved making a bit of a mess.

Several days later my class strode into the room. I took out my scrapfolio to show them my newest creation and their three-day project: The Gratitude Page. Earlier in the year the complaints were more restrained, but our familiarity with one another allowed for the more effusive comments to shoot at me. "We are NOT in kindergarten!" Mason would howl. "This is stupid, Bucon," Nick would mumble under his breath. Others shook their heads and complained that they "can't write that much!" Some laughed and seemed excited.

"Patience, people," I chuckled as I set my Gratitude Page atop a table where they would examine my handiwork at length. "You will all be fine. I promise."

♦

Mom and I met Chris at 18th Street Center on Monday afternoon. Her friend Chris was already busy at work slicing up cucumber stock donated by local produce stores into small pieces, mixing in some chopped onion and vinegar for a nice side salad for the afternoon crowd. Mom and I went to the back room where we grabbed a green and maroon apron to wear as part of the uniform. Mom walked into the kitchen to saddle up beside Chris where they would both decide how she could jump into the day's activities. I stood behind her while waiting for Sally and Chet to finish their discussion about the chafing pan and the mixture of spaghetti, beef, and seasoned tomato sauce which steamed atop a stainless steel prep table. I wondered what adventure Sally would have for me. She always had some strange "A.J. job" whenever I came. One afternoon she had me break apart frozen fish fillets, offering me yellow plastic kitchen gloves in a vain effort to prevent the fish smell from latching onto me. Another time I spent an hour counting and sorting donated hams in the frigid confines of the walk-in freezer. Sally always smiled and accepted my complaining in exchange for a job well done.

"Oh, AJ! You're back for the summer?" Sally announced from the opposite end of the kitchen.

"Yep. Back to enjoy a little down time," I said as I wrapped the apron cords around my waist to show my readiness to work.

"Then school was good?"

"Oh, yeah. Good as always. I'm just glad another year is over." I chuckled.

"Well, I'm glad you're here to help. That's so nice of you." She made her way across the kitchen to give me a big hug. "Let me show you what I need you to do."

I don't know how Sally had this job all ready for me, but I still followed her back to the storage area where I rediscovered the many rows of long white shelves which line the narrow hallway. Many of the once full shelves were nearly empty while others contained a hodge-podge mixture of canned goods, baking supplies, and pasta boxes.

"A.J., come on back here," Sally asked as we made our way past the long rows of shelves. Near the back at the delivery area, Sally pointed to six tall stacks of boxes, explaining that she wanted me to unpack the cans and place them on the shelves while moving stock from one shelf to the next. "So the cans of peaches will go where all the canned fruit is but move the smaller cans to this shelf and organize them first. Once you finish that, break down all of the boxes and toss them in the dumpster out back. I can use you in the kitchen after that."

I gave the six stacks of boxes a quick up-down, noting that they looked as if they could tip over at any moment. "So, this is a lot of food, Sally. Did you order these? I thought you received donations."

"We do take donations, but when the shelves don't have enough to serve everyone who needs us, we have to buy supplies."

"So these six stacks will last a while, huh?"

Sally shook her head. "Those stacks may last about two weeks." Sally left me there to ponder the enormity of, not my task, but the enormity of the task 18th Street Center undertakes to serve the poor. I began my work, silently moving all of the cans, organizing them, imagining how they would be put to use.

◆

"So this is how I need you to paint your hand," I explained to the class. I took a brush, faux-dipping into paint, then spread the imaginary and invisible color across my hand. They just stared at me, wanting no part of this activity and my explanation.

"Chance, can you come up here to help me out?" I had to begin with Chance, one of the leaders, the top dawg, the team captain, the soul. If I can engage Chance without a problem, everyone else will follow. Chance was always good at putting himself out there. He lumbered willingly to the front of the room where I had spread a plastic tablecloth on the table to catch drops of paint.

"O.K., so roll up your sleeves as high as possible so that you don't get any paint on your clothing." He did this, carefully pushing his CCHS sleeves up his arms. "Now, Chance. I need you to take one of the foam brushes and pick up some of the paint." He was a pro. Chance filled it up with paint, leaving a nice big glob on the brush. He looked at me for the next step. "Now, paint all over the palm side." Chance laughed and started painting, coloring his palm with the red tempura paint. "Now the fingers. Get the fingers!" I was obsessing over Chance creating a great first example. "A little there. More there. Ease up. You don't want it too messy." I was a madman, so I am sure he was glad to make it to the end. I showed him how to make a solid handprint by pushing down my weight atop my flattened palm on a tan sheet of cardstock paper. Chance went ahead and did the same himself. After a few moments of pushing and applying pressure to his fingers, he eased up all on his own and I said, "Slowly pull the paper from the back of your hand." As Chance did this, he found a big red handprint on the paper. "Hold it up, Chance. I need a picture."

He held it up. "I made a turkey." Everyone joined Chance in his laughter.

"Yeah. Yeah. Yeah. It's a turkey." I shook my head, conceding innocently that this is what he had created.

They all came up then, two by two painting their hands, making a testament to the individuals they were right there, right at this moment. It was a chaotic mess with students making their hand prints then laughing as they ran to Ann Kahle's room to wash off the excess paint in the sink. Once everyone was back in the room, we sat beside the handprints which lined the chalkboard to dry as I showed them the next stage of The Gratitude Page.

♦

I had stacked all of the cans, organized the stragglers, and broken down the boxes. Mom and Chris had completed the two-hundred-plus fruit cups for the meal delivery the next day, sweetened up the bowl of cucumber salad with a touch of sugar, and plated the donated chocolate cake atop serving trays. We all stood ready behind the serving counter, our aprons barely soiled from the afternoon's prep work. Chris stirred the spaghetti, to her right Mom mixed the scalloped potatoes, and beside Mom I manned the cucumber and dessert section. We were all prepared to serve dinner to the local poor who sat in the dining room.

Sally walked out to the front where she began dinner service with a quiet reflection she read from her own folded prayer book. She took time to consider the meaning of this passage, framing her entire pre-meal talk to focus on gratitude. Sally looked out at the crowded dining room, "We need someone to say grace before we eat." She stood quietly as those awaiting the meal looked to one another for someone to volunteer. Eventually one of the regular attendees stood up to make the sign of the cross; everyone followed suit, clasping their hands in prayer and thanksgiving.

"Thank you," Sally announced. "Now let's allow all of the elderly and children up first." With that the dining room became a boisterous crowd which moved into the designated line where the three of us would serve dinner from behind the counter. I stood beside Mom, understanding more and more the importance of gratitude for the food that I have every day, for the shelter over my head, for my opportunities, and for the family and friends I have.

♦

The next day in class we began the final stage of this project. The class searched the internet and their religion notebooks for thoughts and quotations on gratitude, choosing a secular quotation or a religious verse which could be the focus for the scrapfolio page. For my Gratitude Page I had chosen an excerpt from Psalm 100:

"Shout for joy to the Lord, all the earth. Worship the Lord with gladness; come before him with joyful songs. Know that the Lord is God. It is he who made us, and we are his; we are his people, the sheep of his pasture. Enter his gates with thanksgiving and his courts with praise; give thanks to him and praise his name."

Once everyone had chosen the quotation or verse which worked for them, I challenged them to consider at least seven to ten aspects of their lives for which they were grateful. Creating a list is pretty easy for most people, but I asked them to compose at least three well-developed sentences for each aspect they identified. Many times we can easily claim we are thankful for this person, for a certain moment, or for our opportunities, but articulating the underlying reason for this gratitude is challenging for most people because typically the reasons often go unsaid. This became a project in articulating the reasons not just tossing out some random thoughts.

This stage took longer than I anticipated as the class struggled finding just the right words, the perfect descriptions, the best characterizations which captured their feelings. Many used this opportunity to dig deep into their hearts and minds for the reasons which they would feel comfortable expressing. I showed them my completed page again and explained how I took what I planned and transcribed it in pen around the very edges of my handprint, creating a swirling design that would require effort from the reader to engage with my page. I cut out parts of the excerpt from Psalm 100 and mounted them on tiny square pieces of paper around the sides in an effort to create an artistic organization for my page.

I do not insist on my students modeling what I do on my pages. I like to show them options, allowing for their own creativity to develop. After all, this is their vision, their voice, their project. We brainstormed other ways of placing our gratitude text on the page, then they instinctually set about completing their pages on their own. I stepped back, watching them reflect, write, and create a beautiful and personal representation of gratitude.

◆

Quite often I look at my hands, flipping from the backs to the palms as I hold them out in front of me. When I am examining the backs of my hands, I stretch my fingers as wide as possible until I can feel the tension in my tendons then slowly release them, eventually squeezing my fingers back into tight fists. I flip my hands over to look at my palms then repeat the same process. I do not know what I am hoping to find among the creases, nicks, scars, bumps, and blemishes. There are no words or pictures embedded in my epidermis, nothing to indicate what my hands have accomplished, what my hands have given, what my hands have received. There is no narrative to explain where I have fallen or how I have picked myself back up again.

I flip them back over again and repeat this same ritual until I feel an energy below the surface which is the result of the fingers stretching and closing, the blood moving throughout my hands. This energy triggers a recollection which speaks to me of what is inside, that which is not apparent on the outside. It is that sense of gratitude for the life that I have experienced that day as well as on the numerous days which preceded it. It is the appreciation for the people and opportunities with which I have been blessed. It is the satisfaction that I have expressed my gratitude through my words and actions to those with whom I share this world.

10

Snowflakes of Glue and Love

The second Saturday after Thanksgiving began as a cold morning, one typical of the northern climate to which I had returned. I relish those Saturday mornings in the fall and winter when I can sleep a while longer than I normally would, turning over in my bed to shut off the internal alarm which has silently awoken me. I can wrap myself in the bedspread and an extra layer of blankets while drifting off for another hour or two of sleep that I lost the previous week. The day is one for decompression, a day to sort through the cobwebs of my life outside of school, beyond the ringing bells, a short distance from papers which will not be read until Sunday evening (if then at all). The day is sacrosanct for most people. It is "me" time, a time for reading a book while drinking a cup of fresh brewed coffee before it has a chance to grow cold, a time for mindful reflection without worrying about the second hand of the clock moving forward.

A.J. Bucon

This Saturday morning was different.

Today was the second half of the CCHS Canned Food Drive, the collection day. The frigid air enveloped all of the freshmen, sophomores, parents, teachers, and community volunteers who gathered outside of the Saint Michael Parish Angelus Center. We all rolled out of bed a little later than we normally would on a typical school day, arriving early to separate into small groups who would canvas the adjacent neighborhoods where bags had been left during the first half of this service project. Jeff Smay climbed aboard the back end of a pick-up truck to lead the gathering in prayer. Wisps of air rose from Jeff's mouth as he asked God for a blessing to keep everyone safe throughout the morning and to instill in all of us the spirit of understanding for what we were about to do. Across Wheeling other groups gathered at Saint Vincent School in Elm Grove and at community shelters in Warwood and Bethlehem where they would also begin this city-wide trek to gather canned goods and supplies for Catholic Charities' Neighborhood Center.

I worked inside the Angelus Center where I would man the freshman table with Jamie Campbell. In less than half an hour students would be returning to this location where they would unload countless brown paper bags overflowing with ramen noodles, canned soup, spaghetti sauce, cereal, and fruit cups among numerous other items to be transported to 18th Street Center once we had completed a rudimentary tabulation of the number of items each class had collected. Jamie and I would lead the parents in sorting the cans, boxes, and glass items into plastic crates on loan from Jebbia's Food Market for this particular day.

My Corner of the World

Once the bags started arriving, an enthusiastic chaos ensued. Jamie manned the tabulation sheet as parents and I frantically dove through the bags, pulling out items, keeping a running tally in our heads while transferring the cans to one crate and the boxes and glass items to another. "Thirty!" "Ten!" "Twenty-five!" We would yell out the counts from every brown bag to Jamie in a fun competition with the volunteers manning the sophomore tables at the far end of the room in the Angelus Center. Jamie would laugh then repeat each number as she wrote it down. Empty brown paper bags were randomly thrown to the area behind all of the tables where another volunteer would attempt to organize them, preparing each stack as back up once all of the crates would eventually overflow. Chaos ruled as many of us became bug-eyed at the constant barrage of bulging paper bags exuberant students were carefully carrying into the Angelus Center. As empty areas on the tables became less and less available, students began depositing the bags in front of the tables rather than standing there and waiting for us to finish so that they could head back out to collect more donations. A mountain of generous donations appeared in the span of an hour, slowly growing taller and spreading across the Angelus Center floor until we all became lost amid the colorful and glorious clutter.

Outside of the Angelus Center, SUVs, mini-vans, and cars with exhausts filling the cold air awaited the small groups of students, ready for parents to drive the young people to streets not yet covered on the yellow highlighted maps. They exited the parking lot, all heading in opposite directions down National Road to collect bags from areas noted on the maps. Separate pick-up trucks parked near the rear of the

Angelus Center where crates from inside were painstakingly loaded under the supervision of diligent fathers who used their knowledge of effective packing and organization of vehicles to ensure that the valuable goods made the trip to the Neighborhood Center without incident. At 18th Street Center another group of organized volunteers separated the cans, boxes, and jars into more specific categories, placing them on the soon-to-be-filled shelves I had once organized last summer.

Despite the frigid air that Saturday morning, a warmth slowly filled the air as the young students, teenagers who can be so much of themselves if not pointed towards better horizons, teenagers who need an occasional nudge in the direction of altruism, embraced this moment with an energy and enthusiasm which forced any complacency or angst regarding an early Saturday morning school project to the background. Having volunteered at 18th Street Center all of those summers with Mom gave me a unique insight into just how all of these generous donations of time and talent would affect the poor in this area. As I looked around at the students who helped to clean up remaining brown bags and to restore the tables and chairs in the Angelus Center to their original rows, I saw Sam, Lucas, and Tasha, three freshmen in my English I class, who were participating in this service project for the first time. Did they understand the magnitude of what the entire CCHS student body had accomplished with this project? Was there a way we could add an epilogue to this story for them? Was there a way I could merge their world, the world of Mom, the world of those who work at 18th Street Center, and the world of those who desperately depend on their services?

My Corner of the World

Could I create an experience of all of these worlds meeting together as one, leaving a lasting impression on all of those involved?

I was going to need some glue and a bunch of patience.

♦

The Monday after the Saturday morning collection school returned to its routine with teachers closing out the first semester with final lessons then beginning preparation for exams which the students would take before Christmas. My English I class had recently completed the reading of excerpts from Homer's *The Odyssey*, and I was not quite ready to dive into any other complicated unit prior to the exam. I had something totally different in mind. So our small class said our morning prayer then settled in for a discussion about our weekend.

Sam spoke up right away, stating the obvious as he would always do. "Mr. Bucon, I saw you at the canned food drive on Saturday."

"I know, right? I saw you there, too. I saw a bunch of you there. That was kind of a crazy morning!"

"I cannot believe how many bags we picked up," Sam added. "My arms were so sore that afternoon."

"I know what you mean, Sam." I shook my head to add my pain to Sam's. "I had to go through all of those bags to count how many items the sophomores collected! I never saw so many cans!"

"Mr. Bucon," Lucas interrupted. "I have a question, but I am not sure you can answer this." Lucas was nervous about the question so he anxiously looked about the classroom at his friends for approval, eventually ending up at me to ask, "How many cans did we collect? I mean, I just want to see if we beat the sophomores." Tasha and Sam joined Lucas in their own silent plea to know the answer, speaking with curiosity in their eyes.

I laughed. "Lucas, I honestly cannot remember. They collect all of the numbers in top secret, and I guess someone will let us know the overall winner this week." That answer was not what the class wanted to hear. They were so proud of the work they did on Saturday and were anxious to know if the reward of a "dress-down" day for the winning class was in the cards for them. "You know that there is so much more to what you did on Saturday than possibly beating the sophomores." I slowly surveyed them, hoping to subtly change the topic to another avenue for discussion. "Right, Tasha? Sam?"

Tasha rolled her eyes and slid down in her seat, not ready or willing to answer that question. She looked from side to side at the students around her then offered a mumbled, "I guess."

Sam raised his hand and smiled, keenly aware about where I was going with the point I was making. "Mr. Bucon, I think I can answer your question."

Everyone sighed at Sam's enthusiasm to provide us all with the obvious answer. "Go ahead, Sam. Tell us what you think."

"Central really helped many of the poor people in Wheeling by collecting all of that food."

"Are any of you aware of what they do at 18th Street Center?" I asked, wondering if anybody had been there to volunteer. Several mentioned that they had helped with the spaghetti dinner fund-raiser and had helped serve food once or twice. Most just looked around as Tasha did earlier, unaware of what transpires there so I talked to them about some of the times that I spent over the summer volunteering while home from North Carolina. I told them about Mom and Chris and how they prepared the lunches which would be delivered to people who were shut-in, incapable of leaving their homes on a regular basis to secure a regular meal in the way we could open our refrigerators to find a snack. I spoke of Sally, Sister Constance, and Sister Teresa, explaining how all of them made sure that there was always a nice dinner served on a daily basis at 18th Street. I opened a door to a world that many of them had only heard in passing; they did not truly understood the impact the center has on the community.

"So this is what I was thinking. How about we do something really nice for the people who receive those lunches that the volunteers make for them? How about we do something that helps us to remember the important part of the Christmas season?" I went around behind my desk to retrieve a folded red piece of construction paper. I held up the paper, flipping it over so that the class could appreciate this handmade Christmas card. On the front was a white snowflake. This was not just any kind of snowflake; it was one of those for which I had folded a square sheet of paper several times then took a pair of scissors to cut out large and tiny parts of the paper. Once it was unfolded, I had glued it on the front. Inside the card I presented my handwritten note:

"When they saw the star, they rejoiced exceedingly with great joy." Matthew 2:10
I hope that you have a Merry Christmas and keep Jesus in your heart.

A.J., CCHS

Many of their eyes lit up at the thought of making a Christmas card for someone they did not know. Cole, one of the more stoic and "cool" guys in the class, flipped his head back, nodded affirmatively, and then confidently boasted, "I can do one of those." Everyone followed his lead. Tasha looked at her friend who sat beside her and smiled.

"Now, before everyone gets too excited, I need to explain what this entails." They winced incredulously, just as my juniors winced when I explained the *The Canterbury Files* project, just as my seniors winced for The Gratitude Page for the scrapfolio. "Did I forget to mention how many people receive these meals? I mean, we need to have one for each person."

The class looked at one another to see if it were possible that they had once again missed some information their teacher had shared. Lucas, a look of trepidation covering his face, provided the response for everyone. "Uh, Mr. Bucon. I believe you forgot to tell us that."

"Oh, no problem." I leisurely began to count the small group of students around the room. "One, two, three, four -"

"Ten, Bucon." Cole deadpanned. "There are ten of us."

"Thanks, Cole." I wrote the number of students down on a sheet of paper. "There are 250 people who receive these meals on a daily basis, everyone." I wrote that number down. "So 250 divided by 10 is-," I feigned doing long division, beginning to reach annoyingly for a calculator on my desk.

"Twenty-five," Lucas frowned, exasperated at my apparent lack of simple division skill.

My Corner of the World

"Thanks, Lucas! You all are going to be so good at this! I can tell! So each one of you will be making *only* twenty-five handmade Christmas cards for this project! Now let me write each step of the project on the board."

I had my doubts about whether my eagerness and affability would last the duration of this project. Their eyes spoke volumes about the grand scope of this project to them. Sam just laughed with excitement as he turned to look at the board, Lucas dropped his head back to look at the ceiling and mumbled quietly to himself, Cole sat stone-faced, chewing on some invisible gum he had in his mouth, and poor Tasha slid down in her desk again while her friend giggled at her.

♦

I have a huge collection of Christmas music in my iTunes library and an ancient CD wallet overstuffed with CDs from when I would collect them regularly. I cannot dive into the Christmas spirit soon enough once November arrives, anxiously picking out some Christmas songs long before a turkey is even chosen for Thanksgiving dinner. My eclectic selection allows me to find just the right song to accompany my frame of mind on any given occasion. The Sunday after the food collection I was browsing through the iTunes store in search of some music to capture the underlying spirit of the project I planned with my class of freshmen. I found Steven Curtis Chapman's song "Christmas Card" in the middle of his CD *Joy*. It was the perfect song for me, the perfect song for our class, the perfect song to frame the journey on which we were about to embark.

When class met on the first day after the big project announcement, I spoke to the students again about understanding for whom we were creating these cards. "I know this is going to be a fun project, and, yes, Lucas, it will also be a great deal of work." I glanced at all of them, then dropping the jokey side of my personality, I thoughtfully described the people who would be receiving these cards. "Many of the people who receive the daily delivery of the meals do so because they may not be as fortunate as many of us are. Some people may not have the money to afford more than one good meal a day. Others live alone. Think about what it would be like to not have any family around anymore, to not feel comfortable enough to walk outside on the street or down a hallway by yourself. Imagine that the only human contact you have on a daily basis is the person who is bringing you this meal."

I looked around at them as each student carefully listened to my emotional portrayal of the lives of the people we were helping. It is so important for young people to develop and nurture the compassionate side of themselves, to understand that not everyone has the same life as each one of us has, to recognize that we do have the ability to affect some change in their lives. "Put yourself in one of those person's shoes. Imagine what it would be like to receive a wonderful card from a young person like you. Imagine that the person places the card on a table so he or she can see it every day."

Sam piped up. "Mr. Bucon, how are these people going to get the cards?"

"Honestly, Sam, I am not entirely sure. Why do you ask?"

"I just think it would be nice if they received it really close to Christmas. It will *mean more* then."

"That is a great idea, Sam. Let me check with the people who are in charge of the meal program to see if the cards can be delivered with the meals."

On that note, we dove into the project. I gave the students a collection of bible verses related to Christmas that I had compiled for them. "I need you to look through the verses that I have on this page to see if you can find one that will be perfect to put on each of your cards along with a special wish." Tasha and her friend meticulously read the list together, talking about the reasons each liked or disliked certain quotations. Cole looked at Sam, Lucas, and some other students then asked me if it would be OK to use their cell phones to find their own if they did not want to use one of mine. I told them that would be fine as we all settled into writing the verse and a warm, thoughtful message in as neat a manner as possible, using blue or black ink, a sense of proportion on the page, and a good-faith desire that we were all going to do our best.

The next phase began as soon as the students returned to class the next day. My earnest elves gathered around me, the Papa Elf in our Snowflake Workshop. I did my best to brace my cordial and nurturing persona against my darker Scrooge self, the one who desired perfectly folded papers and carefully cut divots of numerous varieties which were well-spaced throughout each snowflake. "OK, gang. Here we go." I began to model the process for them while watching how all of the students completed their first individual folds in their own unique and imperfect manner. "Take the paper and fold it in half, carefully making sure the edge of one side touches the edge of the opposite side." Some folds were perfect, others were slightly askew, and a couple were nearly an inch past an even fold. Sometimes we need to let perfection go, right? Particularly when it comes to Christmas. Particularly when making snowflakes, two hundred and fifty snowflakes to be more precise. "Now, everyone, we will take our scissors and cut a little triangle out of the side." Maybe it was the blunted safety scissors, but we truly dropped into low gear then. Every single cut I asked them to model took at least a minute per person. Time slowed for all of us as tiny pieces of paper flew up into the air and floated gently to the tile floor. After fifteen or so minutes, we developed a nice rhythm as the folded papers began to materialize into the seeds of a future snowflake with more diverse cuts: triangles, rectangles, and looping ovals. Once it appeared as if everyone had enough cuts, I shouted, "Okay, everyone! Slowly open your paper to see your first snowflake!" This funny group of freshman all marveled at how great some snowflakes were while cackling at the odd shapes of others. "OK, write your name on the back of yours! Everyone has twenty-four more to do!" With wide eyes and a sigh, the gang began to fold the next paper.

 The snowflake phase took more than a couple of days. By the third day Papa Elf had grown a bit grumpy about the tiny scattered pieces of paper all over the floor at the end of each class and with the lack of focus some of the elves began to develop after having cut so many snowflakes for so long. The camaraderie in the Snowflake Workshop was palpable with Cole helping Tasha put the finishing touches on her snowflakes and

Sam keeping Lucas's concentration on his snowflakes rather than jabbering about what he was going to do over Christmas. Seeing them laugh and help one another enabled me to overlook the messy floor and amount of time it took to finally complete this project. Each student had his or her own snowflakes ready to glue to the front of the cards and began the next phase of writing the special message on his or her twenty-five sheets of paper. In fact, in the interest of time (Christmas break was nearly upon us), writing these messages turned out to be good homework for them. As time grew closer to the completion date, we used innumerable glue sticks to finish all two-hundred and fifty Christmas cards. Eventually each student placed all of his or her cards in a gallon-sized zip-lock plastic bag with his or her name on it, all set for delivery to 18th Street Center. We were finished. Well, not entirely.

♦

Several days before final exams began at Central, my freshman class, Becky Sancomb, and I made a field trip four blocks away from the school to 18th Street Center. As we finished the last of the Christmas cards, I informed the class of a secret on which I had been sitting for a while. I had made arrangements with P.J., the services coordinator at 18th Street Center, for all of us to tour and hear an in-depth explanation of all that this location does for the community. It would prove to be a fitting conclusion to both the canned food drive and Christmas card projects for these young people, hopefully allowing them to understand more deeply how their service impacts people.

The glorious morning served to magnify the enthusiasm and anticipation of all of the students as we high-tailed it down the sidewalks of Wheeling to 18th Street Center. A level of uncertainty rode the undercurrent of our excitement as many of the class seemed uneasy about bridging the comfortable gap between helping the poor from the outside and moving among where many of these souls would travel themselves. This is where I made my first connection and where they would make theirs. With each person carrying his or her bag of Christmas cards, we walked through the front door and into a world that was decidedly different from the one which we had left, one which would prove to be as worldly an educational experience as any I could offer in the classroom. A few people from the community who had stopped at the center that morning to eat breakfast, to take a shower, to request a change of clothes, or to simply rest sat around the lobby watching as our group made its way through the front door to the dining room.

P.J. greeted us when we arrived, and (knowing that we were on a tight schedule with other classes to attend at school) he began his tour without delay. As a teacher I am always concerned about having my student's undivided attention, constantly reviewing directions or checking for understanding. Most adult attention spans last about eight seconds so questions of whether or not my students are fully grasping what I have placed in front of them fill the back of my mind. As I watched my class that morning, they were clearly engaged, filled with an inquisitiveness about just what happens here.

We stood there in the dining room as P.J. called our attention to the kitchen area, the same kitchen area where Mom had spent so many years of her life preparing fruit cups for the meal delivery or serving dinner to the poor who would come for a meal every afternoon. P.J. made sure to ask if anyone had ever worked in the kitchen or served food here. Several of us raised our hands and shared the times we had volunteered. P.J. thanked us for what we had done then led us to several rows of stainless steel tables in an area adjacent to the dining room. The group of freshmen, the ones who were so talkative and silly while making the Christmas cards, were engrossed in P.J.'s explanation as he talked, listening to his informative explanation of every aspect of the Neighborhood Center, eyes moving around the room to imagine how it all would be used.

Atop the steel tables were stacks and stacks of food items, the very ones which had been collected during the recent canned food drive. Shelves also full of donated food bordered the tables. Enraptured by the enormity of it all, we stood in the midst of all of this generosity as P.J. explained how 18th Street Center was truly dependent on the yearly canned food drive as it made up one-sixth of the total contributions for the year, filling the shelves with much needed food supplies during the cold winter months. He explained how bags were packed with essential items and delivered to those in most need during the holiday season. The sense of pride and accomplishment swelled with each breath the students took. They were a part of all of this, they were witnessing the impact they had made, and they were considering what more they could do.

As the tour came to an end, we all gathered for the presentation of the Christmas cards. Before taking pictures of each student presenting his or her cards, P.J. made an announcement, a final bow to place on our gift. "I want to thank you again for these cards and for taking the time to visit with us today. Mr. Bucon and I have made arrangements so that your cards will be accompanying each meal delivered on Christmas Day." He smiled while locking eyes with each of them. "Again, thank you so much for your hard work on this project." The class quickly looked around at one another, beaming and nodding proudly at this special announcement. I asked them to begin, one at a time, to carry their cards up to present P.J. and to shake his hand while posing for a picture. Each one politely took his or her turn. Sam began then came Lucas with the rest following suit, each taking a beat to appreciate the moment. Becky took a group picture at the end, one in which we all widely grinned, not only for different personal reasons but for the completion of one common goal.

Our group said farewell to P.J. and the staff, thanking them for the opportunity to visit this morning. As we left the dining room and entered the lobby area to the front door, some of the people who were there earlier remained in the same seats, joined by a few others who arrived while we were touring the center and presenting our cards. Sam smiled, gave a quick wave, and said, "Goodbye! I hope you have a nice Christmas!" Several of the people replied with their own thanks and a wave, leading to more of the class responding in kind, offering "goodbyes" and "have a nice days" of their own.

That day our class saw the result of our efforts, not just the Saturday morning collection of the canned goods or the crazy and chaotic creation of Christmas cards but the ability we have as individuals, both young and old, to make a difference in a world both beyond and part of our own.

My Corner of the World

Armed with brown paper bags, red and green construction paper, ink pens, a box of glue sticks, boundless energy, and a treasure chest of love, we rediscovered the importance of never being alone, never entirely being unto one's self, particularly when we can make a connection with others.

11

Midterms

Anyone who has been to school should know what midterms are. Each person, whether he or she be student or teacher, recognizes the anxiety associated with this type of assessment. Teachers use these stopping points midway through an entire school year to discover whether or not anything from the last five months has "stuck." Are students retaining any of the knowledge or skills addressed over that time? Students can quite often be found sprinting from locker to locker, from friend to stranger, in an effort to make sure they have all of their bases covered. Quite often they carry a handful of teacher-printed study guides completed individually or with "assistance" from other students.

I had not administered an official midterm in well over a decade. Two basic school schedules are the year-long model and the block schedule. Throughout my years at Central I matriculated under the former by traversing seven classes a day from August until June. I began teaching in North Carolina on the year-long schedule, preparing for

English I, English III, Theater I, Theater II, and Advanced Theater for an entire year. Imagine the excitement of a new teacher who has five different preparations! Luckily I possessed a youthful exuberance which gave me the energy to endure this schedule of classes. About seven years later, Wilson County Schools moved to a block schedule. Students now had four ninety minute classes a day for one semester, eventually taking eight classes in a school year. As a teacher I would have three classes a day with one planning period. Non-teachers may say that my life was easier with this change. Going from forty-minute classes to ninety minute classes necessitates a change in the way a person teaches whether a teacher is ready for it or not. It was this change that allowed me to expand my repertoire which depended less and less on direct instruction and lecturing and to move more towards student-centered activities that have become the heart of what I strive to accomplish today in my classroom. On the block schedule we had final exams at the end of each semester. If the class happened to have a state End-of-Course exam, students sat for a high-stakes exam to earn class credit. Other classes which did not have a state-mandated EOC offered students a reprieve from the pressure of the lengthy standardized assessment. Regardless of the exam situation, I needed to evaluate students, not just on specific content they had learned, but more importantly, to me and my students, the skills they had developed.

My homecoming to Central brought with it a return to the year-long schedule, the multiple preparations, the shorter classes, and the midterms as well as final exams. I had been on the block schedule for so long that the transition back to the year-long schedule proved difficult. I wanted to retain my philosophy of student-centered activities but was challenged with the time and pacing adjustments of this schedule. By the end of the first semester, my students kept asking me about my midterms. How many questions will be on the midterm? Would they be a mixture of multiple choice, matching, fill in the blank, and true or false? When are they getting a study guide? Will the class be reviewing?

◆

My freshmen rolled into class on exam day, a bit uncertain regarding what to expect. We had just completed the Catholic Charities Neighborhood Center Christmas card project and, prior to that, *The Odyssey*. Earlier that week I told them that our exam would involve some thoughtful personal reflection and, of course, some writing. I added that there was little they could do to truly prepare for it other than bringing a pen and some paper. Confusion enveloped their countenances as they saw a television and DVD player on a media cart standing front and center of our semi-circle.

We all sat down, said our prayer at the beginning of class, and then proceeded to reflect about the last few months. We began to talk about all of the different selections we read first semester, the ones they enjoyed and the ones they did not like at all. We shared our recent memories of the card creation and delivery day at 18th Street Center. Everyone joined in the conversation as each person freely related what he or she had accomplished.

"Now," I offered as I moved toward the media cart. "I have something I want to show all of you. I made a little video of our Christmas card project. I was so proud of all of your efforts and how much you helped other people." Lucas, Sam, Tasha, and all of the students in the class sat up a little higher in their seats and leaned in to watch the video. I had used the Steven Curtis Chapman song, the one which inspired my development of this project we had just completed. The song "Christmas Card" served as a backdrop to a pictorial narrative of our project from the early snowflake cutting, to the pasting on the cards, along the walk through Wheeling, and during P.J.'s informative presentation at 18th Street Center. They all loved the video and asked if they could see it one more time. "Well, we need to take our exam first. Let's go ahead and take out your pens and papers." Of course, the borrowing ensued, but they were all set to go when I distributed the exam.

As I gave the students each a sheet of paper, they all read both prompts I had written there while intently looking up and down at me then at one another. "I am going to read each prompt aloud, stopping to see if there are any questions. Both of these prompts will be written as well-developed essays. Please do your best to recall what we have discussed this semester about sentence writing, paragraph development, and organization." They all nodded affirmatively, understanding what we had established as expectations for writing throughout the year thus far. "Prompt One: Choose any selection we have read this year and develop a thoughtful essay in which you discuss the specific content regarding the selection and literary devices the author uses while offering the message or insight you gained from reading this selection." Pause. "Any questions?" Everyone confidently shook their heads. "Prompt Two: Regarding the Christmas card project and our trip to 18th Street Center, discuss what you learned about how the center helps the community, how the Central canned food drive impacts the center, and, finally, what you learned personally about yourself and others from the completion of this project. Any questions?" Again, they just shook their heads. "Are you sure?"

"Mr. Bucon," Sam interrupted and laughed. "I think we have it. Can we just get started? We have a lot of writing to do."

"Sure, Sam. Good luck, everyone."

My students dove into the work, much as a person who had been laboring in the hot sun would dive into a refreshing pool. They swam and swam, delving into selections like Richard Connell's "The Most Dangerous Game," Toni Cade Bambara's "Blues Ain't No Mockin' Bird," and Homer's *The Odyssey*, each one choosing that which connected to them the most. They immersed themselves deeply in their memories of the trip to 18th Street Center while sharing more details than even I remembered myself. Not one person appeared to doubt what he or she was writing on the paper. No one came close to finishing until class was nearly over. Was this a typical midterm that they had expected? Probably not. This assessment did afford all of us an opportunity to measure how much we have grown academically and just how much about life we had learned since the beginning of the year. These two essays provided me with valuable insights into how my students think, what my students believe, and how they relate to the world around them.

♦

Emily, J.T., Mason, and the rest of the seniors had finished up first semester in quite the impressive manner by exploring some challenging nonfiction selections, writing numerous rhetorical analyses, reading Ilibagiza's *Left to Tell*, reflecting in their journals, and, of course, completing various pages of their scrapfolio. Once again, I struggled with what to do for the midterm exam, wavering between what the students had traditionally expected and what I found to be more conclusive when it comes to a summative assessment. I could easily create a midterm exam full of rhetorical terms, I could require them to write yet another analysis, I could ask questions about *Left to Tell*, and I could mix in some Sadlier vocabulary for good measure. I could do all of this just to create a midterm that the students would hate. To what end though? Had we not mastered all of these items on numerous occasions? Would it make a difference if we did a combination of all of these one more time? Surely there was something more cumulative and more authentic we could attempt.

"Let me explain what we are going to do with the midterm exam," I began near the end of class about two or three days before exams started. They took out their notebooks to write down everything I would tell them. I went through my thought process with them, referencing all of the work we had accomplished first semester, thoughtfully explaining what I could do with the various types of questions and prompts. I took them down memory lane again as I retold the origins of the scrapfolio and how I used it in my English class in North Carolina for a final presentation grade. I recalled how thoughtful and interesting these presentations were and that I believed we could recreate the same experience here for our midterms.

"So what are you saying, Uncle A.J.?" J.T. asked, the first of the class to adopt Emily's family name for me. "Are we just presenting our scrapfolios for our midterm?" I can recall the looks of skepticism arising again as the class looked at me in disbelief.

"Well, yeah," I answered. "I think that is what we are going to do."

Some people balked, saying that they were not presenting their scrapfolio to anyone and that this was a stupid idea. Others pushed back by making the case about how easy it would be, and that they would only be presenting them to the class. They would have no exam, no study guide to complete, no review sessions, no test to take. At the heart of the dissent was the relevant fact that public speaking is many people's number one fear, beyond even death. I was not just asking them to give a speech about an inconsequential or random topic; I was asking them to share the personal aspects of their scrapfolio, their thoughts about topics we had discussed, their feelings about hobbies, sports, and other activities. We were inching forward slowly here, touching the water with our big toe to register a pool's warmth. As a teacher I am in front of people speaking all of the time, and this has become second nature to me; but for many of these students, public speaking was the most frightening challenge I had presented to them all year. Those who are confident about speaking relished this opportunity while those more ambivalent and fearful only wanted a study guide and multiple choice test.

"Look, all year I have asked you to step out of your comfort zone. We started with the scrapfolio. Remember how many of you hated that? Now some of you really like it."

"I still hate it," Chance barked from the back row. Everyone just laughed so we could move on.

"And honestly, many of you are going to college next year. And do you know what? You better be prepared. I guarantee you will be doing presentations just like this. There will be speeches on content you have learned."

"Come on, Bucon," Mason critiqued from the sidelines. "I don't think we will be doing *scrapfolios* when we are in college." Eyes bounced to me at that point. We all knew he was right.

"Of course, Mason, but scrapfolios *are* what we are doing now. Besides, what you all have done is incredible. So much thought and effort have gone into these that it would be a shame if only you saw what you did."

"I'm just fine with that," Chance grumbled again.

"I know you are, but I'm not." Having said that, we moved into the planning stages of the content that they actually had to share, the length of the presentation, and the manner in which they were to present it. "This will *not* be simply strolling up here to the podium and casually showing us the work you did. You will need to practice and know what you are going to say before you do your presentation. You will be earning a grade on just how well you deliver this."

"What?" Chance laughed from the back. "We have to go up to the podium?" Everyone laughed, knowing that Chance, despite his complaints, was always along for the ride.

♦

My Corner of the World

"Good morning. My name is Emily, and this is my scrapfolio presentation for first semester. I'll begin with my alphabiography." Emily pulled her hair back, opened the scrapfolio so that the class could see, then proceeded to walk slowly around the room to allow everyone to view the design of her alphabiography and the block letters in which the descriptions of herself were so neatly written. She returned to the front of the room where she placed the scrapfolio on the podium. "I would like to share a couple of my letters with you." Emily slowly read the contents in order to make sure the class had the opportunity to hear her. Once she finished, she moved on to her gratitude page, professionally completing the same process over again. The next pages were her "student choice" pages, two pages from the remaining collection of pages Emily had completed. These were the ones she chose to present on her own, the ones she shared by either reading from the paragraphs she had written or by simply pointing out pictures she had mounted while explaining the purpose for including them on this page. A polite and generous round of applause ensued once Emily thanked everyone for their attention.

One by one the students moved to the front of the room as all followed the presentation order we had created days earlier. J.T. followed Emily then Nick followed J.T., each person warming in the presence of the appreciative audience made up of students who loved doing the presentation as well as those who grew more nervous as the list wound down to their name. A community of support arose for one another as they recognized the vulnerability of revealing themselves through the shared scrapfolio pages which offered glimpses into who they were as individuals. They were all connected by the experience as they shared a commonality of travelling the same road together while bearing witness to different views of the world as they perceived it.

After a morning of thoughtful insights, humorous accounts, and reflective reminiscing, the class became more than it had been prior to the presentation. We had moved past the invisible superficiality of our day to day routine. The change was palpable.

"That was kind of cool, Bucon," Mason announced shortly after the last person finished, the comment eliciting affirmative nods from everyone.

"I agree. What was it that all of you liked the most?" I asked to gain more insights for myself as well.

"Well, this was pretty easy to do. I mean, we are just explaining the work that we already did," Mason began.

"Yeah, Mase, but I liked hearing what everyone had to say," J.T. continued. "We see one another every day, and we saw what everyone was working on, but this was different."

"We got to know one another more than we already did." Emily added, looking around the room at different people. Shannon, the student at the beginning of the year who seemed so hesitant and nervous about these new activities back then, nodded in lively affirmation as she smiled at Emily. Others joined her in validating the direction of the discussion.

"I agree with all of you," positing my own observation. "I think it is important to recognize the amount of time and energy that went into the pages you created. I mean, it is not as simple as just making a page. Take your *Left to Tell* pages. You read the book, wrote those journals, came up with your own ideas. The presentations are just the tip of the iceberg here. This really gives you a chance to share what you have accomplished with an audience. I truly thought it was interesting to hear what people selected as their two student choice pages to share. We began to see how one another thinks." I looked around as many began talking among themselves about the presentations. "Why don't we take a beat to share what we liked about one another's presentations?"

The class jumped at this opportunity because so often we rarely have the occasion to compliment one another in this type of setting, so the random accolades, not just from good friend to good friend but from person to person, commenced. The affirmations were a testimony to the validity of this activity as I noticed the class taking more ownership of the overall idea.

"Uncle A.J.," J.T. asked. "Can we do something like this again?"

"Oh, absolutely," I smiled. A seed had been planted and the future was a short way down the road, just around the corner.

12

Cheese

Christmas break proved to be a wonderful opportunity to finally catch my breath after a frenetic first semester marathon that really started nearly eight months earlier. The move from North Carolina to West Virginia transpired so quickly over the summer that I never truly considered the impact of this change and how it affected me on an internal level. The shortening of daylight and dropping in temperature mixing with the colorful holiday decorations and serene musicality of the season created a suitable backdrop for contemplation of my own personal and spiritual growth as well as my long term goals for where I would be professionally.

Back when I made the decision to depart Wilson and the world I had created for myself there, my premise for leaving was rooted in a feeling of professional complacency and a desire to return to home and family in Wheeling. The decision proved to be complicated, but one that in my heart I needed to make. Deep down, I believed by making this choice I would possibly discover different levels of happiness while still retaining the wonderful memories of my life there. I believed that if I made this drastic change, I would find a new contentment in the teaching profession which I seemed to have lost. I believed that I would reconnect with my roots, discovering more about the young man I once was and the adult I had become.

At the halfway point of the school year, my life had changed in ways I somewhat imagined it would. I was enjoying the revitalization of beginning anew here at Central, the openness of the students I was teaching, the new colleagues and friends I was beginning to make, and the comfort of family I had missed for those many years in North Carolina. The road to self-discovery and reinvigoration is continuous and includes twists and turns as well as unexpected detours which can take a traveler down paths he never thought he would journey. Second semester would start soon and doubt would inch its way back into my life as it always seemed to do, forcing me to dig a bit deeper to find more determination and desire than I ever thought I had.

♦

The relaxation over break imbued me with an energy to step right back into second semester as if I had been teaching here all of my life. My freshman class spent quite a bit of time reading William Shakespeare's *The Tragedy of Romeo and Juliet* as humorous frustration would arise from time to time while we enjoyed the challenge of navigating the Bard's beautiful yet challenging language. The juniors spent time reading and analyzing classic British poetry, thoughtfully making their own unique connections to timeless themes of youth, death, and love, before eventually reading William Golding's *Lord of the Flies*. Both groups completed the nice balance of writing and creative projects to which they had grown accustomed during first semester. The seniors began argumentative writing as they read topics about gun control, immigration, and poverty. Despite the typical protestations of second semester seniors, they continued their writing development and completed the Change Your World project, an essay-writing, poster-making, speech-giving, video-creating roller coaster ride, all centering on a current topic of each student's own personal interest, such as binge drinking, world hunger, cell-phone use, social media, or teen suicide. All of the outstanding effort and comradery continued second semester with this class. I was where I wanted to be with my students, continuing to present topics and activities which would allow them to grow, revamping both myself and my teaching style as I continued to rediscover my passion for the classroom.

A school has several hallways, multiple classrooms, and numerous doors, some of which are open and welcoming while others are closed to outsiders. Life in a school mirrors many situations in life. We do not typically find ourselves in environments that are as welcoming and nurturing as we would like. Everyone has different beliefs, styles, expectations, and maps to achieve their own personal goals, so sometimes it is easier to shut our doors to others and focus only on that which is important to us. I have been guilty of shutting my door more times than I am willing to admit. The tension that Monsignor Ostrowski addressed during his homily in the opening staff mass in the school chapel still percolated throughout the school, creating a climate of uncertainty and tension. Despite the impromptu Cathedral meeting with the superintendent, principal, and staff, a palpable angst remained present during hallway conversations and faculty meetings. Multiple unseen camps appeared to be set up whenever we gathered together, groups much like the ones which gathered together in the Cathedral that fall. Issues like copier usage, unit plans, scheduling, and discipline became exacerbated when a conflict of personalities fed the fire.

At the beginning of the year I worried about falling into this fray and taking sides while not knowing or understanding completely the contexts in which many of the conflicts had started and subsequently festered. I chose to remain in my room, work with my students, and avoid this consternation as much as possible. I suppose I did actually become involved back when Julie Shively, the principal, asked me to present my Common Core unit plan to the faculty and later assist those who needed help completing their own units. I wanted to remain comfortably secure where I was as I attempted to straddle a fence between indifference and involvement. With the conflicts continuing, I focused on my classroom as long as I could, concentrating on *Romeo and Juliet* raps, *Macbeth* seminars, and Change Your World videos. Honestly, I find it easier sometimes to simply stake my territory in a world where I have some level of comfort and control.

Monsignor Ostrowski would occasionally find me on his weekly visits. As school pastor he was ultimately responsible for overseeing the school's spiritual mission, so he could always be found once or twice a week walking through the hallways to talk to people or look into classrooms. He is a good man, one who always says "hello" and asks how things are going. Many people ask that question, but so few actually seem to mean it the way Monsignor Ostrowski does. "Do you have a minute, A.J.?" he would ask, motioning toward an empty classroom where we would sit across from each other in student desks. "Tell me, how is everything?"

"My classes are great. We have a wonderful group of students here." I would proceed to tell Monsignor about the activities of one class or would mention certain students and their recent achievements. He would always seem to appreciate any details I would offer.

"How about around the school?" he continued after taking a pause for transition's sake.

"Oh, Monsignor, I really don't feel comfortable talking too much about that." I know that I have an incredible weakness to vent uncontrollably sometimes and was cautious about doing so here. I do not think a cathartic confession of sorts is what he expected. From previous conversations I understood that Monsignor might have recognized me as a fresh pair of eyes to see the situation here at Central, a situation which seemed to be causing such anxiety for the staff. As the school pastor, he had been charged with ensuring that the staff was doing its best to follow the school mission. I wanted to offer him some type of insight, an insight which was as thoughtful and considered as I could muster. I always liked to bring up that homily of his at the opening staff mass, the one which startled me so much on my first day. Monsignor would always smile and nod agreeably as I told him that it was evident to me that there were some unexpected challenges I did not anticipate before arriving here. I would state that the new principal had some good ideas for the school, but a lingering concern remained among people who had been teaching here long before Julie arrived regarding the need or purpose for the changes she was implementing. I could never speak to Monsignor about anyone else's concerns, but I always felt safe in stressing that change is always difficult. When uncertainty appears on the horizon, people grow comfortable in their own individual situations and fear a loss in that which they have personally invested or in that which they perceive as a sense of control.

Monsignor Ostrowski and I would talk for a while, exchange pleasantries, shake hands, and then go our separate ways with both of us understanding the subtext throughout the exchange we had shared. He would continue his walk down the hallway while I would gather myself and head back to the security of my classroom.

◆

Several months into second semester, my outlook would take an abrupt but not an entirely unexpected deviation from where I assumed I would eventually travel. We would have staff meetings in many different locales: the library, a nearby classroom, the Cathedral, and the Great Hall. I always wondered if the meeting place had some connection to the substance of the meeting itself thereby giving me some preconceived and futile comfort in a hopeless attempt to brace myself for whatever would be presented. Julie arranged for this day's meeting to take place on a teacher workday so that we could discuss accreditation procedures. We would meet in the Great Hall where its large tables and spacious confines were more amenable to collaborative work. Oddly enough, Julie sat atop a table looking entirely too comfortable for an early morning meeting. She smiled and welcomed everyone as she showed no wear and tear from the turbulence of three quarters of the school year. A cordiality filled the atmosphere with polarization remaining sidelined while pleasant chit-chat flowed throughout the Great Hall as early attendees welcomed the stragglers.

Julie began earnestly as she concluded welcoming everyone. She emanated a calm imperative while releasing a burden she had been carrying a long time. As Julie gazed around the hall, she began by speaking of change and the challenges that accompany it. She recognized that this had been a difficult two years for everyone. Still perched atop the circular table, our principal spoke of how we could all still come together and achieve great things here at Central. She acknowledged that with any type of change people were going to be uncomfortable. Julie then offered an honest assessment of herself when she spoke of how there are times when she wanted to be "someplace else." Looking directly at us then beyond us, she spoke of a "cabin in the mountains by a lake," an unspecified locale that was calm and serene, a setting ideal for her, her husband, and her cat. "That is my perfect place. Sometimes I wish I could just run away to a place like this." Julie smiled at the thought of being there, then she quietly transitioned into the accreditation discussion. We all took a deep breath and followed her to the task at hand.

At the time I did not know what to make of all of this. Julie, a retired Air Force officer, someone who valued discipline, a leader who seemed locked into the technical and specific, a person who was not without her own compassion, an individual with her own faults, had spoken in an unanticipated manner that morning. She had bravely revealed a side of herself as she conceded that a path she was traveling was not one which she had envisioned. This was an awkward moment, but it was also a genuine one, simply because many of us could feel a kinship beyond the struggles of a world which may or may not be one of our own making but one that is ours nonetheless.

Several weeks later, Julie resigned.

♦

Every time I replayed my personal narrative of these events and my subsequent grappling with the aftermath, fragments of another time popped into my mind. When I taught in Wilson County, teachers struggled during the transition from the year-long schedule to the 4 X 4 block schedule. Everyone had this vision of what the school should be and how a daily schedule should run. Entwined with the adjustment to a radically different schedule was the necessity for a change in pedagogy. Whatever style of teaching a person had adopted necessitated modification as each and every teacher needed to adapt to the abruptness of the shift. It was not easy for many. I remember my principal distributing a book the Central Office had purchased for all of the schools: Dr. Spencer Johnson's *Who Moved My Cheese?* Johnson's book was measuredly smaller than a typical book; the title was splayed across the front with a triangular piece of cheese supplanting the "V" in the title. This book was the kind which could be completed in an hour or two sitting. My students would say they would like to read a book like this. I can see their eyes lighting up, pointing at it, and yelling, "Yeah, why we can't read *that* book?" Small books can be overlooked as being simplistic, but there is nothing simple about the contents in this book.

My Corner of the World

Johnson uses a parable as the foundation for his book. Four characters live in a maze where they all discover a large chunk of cheese. Two of the characters, Hem and Haw, are "little people" who move their homes as close to the cheese as possible, believing that it will always be there and making it the center of their world. The two other characters, Scurry and Sniff, are mice who know that the cheese will not be there forever as everyone continues to eat it. Hem and Haw fail to see the cheese becoming progressively smaller until one day the cheese is gone. Scurry and Sniff are fine because they knew this day would come and were discovering cheese elsewhere. Hem and Haw were unprepared and played victims in a situation they created themselves as they blamed someone else for "moving" their cheese.

Upon learning of Julie's resignation, I was definitely some amalgamation of Hem and Haw and Scurry and Sniff. Anger and frustration permeated every aspect of my life. Why had I returned from North Carolina to this? I simply wanted to enjoy teaching again beyond the frustration and lack of motivation I had once felt at Fike High School, but my eyes were so locked on the "cheese" here that I did not see what was going on around me. I was so enthralled in the novelty of returning to Central, of beginning the second half of my career with more knowledge and wisdom than I had when I left West Virginia for North Carolina twenty years earlier. I never thought the rekindled emotion and passion that burned in my heart would die. I never believed change would come in this manner, so sharply and quickly. When the person who hired me left a handful of months before school was adjourned for the summer, I instinctively felt as if the foundation I was building as the next stage of my life was ready to crumble. Initially I was annoyed at Julie for her decision, frustrated with my colleagues and this climate for allowing this situation to boil to this point, and angry at myself for every choice I had made since the previous spring when I accepted this position.

Eventually I began to shake off my feelings of doom. I chose to accept my anger and frustration as being real, but I wanted to focus on moving forward in life with a positivity I still possessed. Becky took the reins of Central for the remainder of the school year and eventually accepted the position as official principal. I returned to focusing on my students with all of our reading and writing, collaboration and scrapfolios. I chose to move past the first draft of my own narrative in order to rediscover my original "cheese." Truthfully I had found a personal renewal teaching here and was extremely happy with what was transpiring in my classroom and of my students' progress and creativity. I found contentment with reestablishing my home here in a place I had left decades ago. Perhaps the original goal I had was an intangible one, one not made up of the actual people around me but one more about the invisible yet perceptible connections among us all, one not erected as a renovated building with decorated classrooms but one of what transpires within its walls. Perhaps my cheese had not been moved at all.

13
Git 'Er Done

"Good morning, everyone! Today we are going to start the project all of you have joyously anticipated!" My senior class dutifully retrieved their notebooks from beneath their desks, quietly sat up to look at the smart board, clicked the tops of their pens in unison, and cordially smiled while awaiting my introduction.

"We are about to start on the senior research project," I began as I pulled enthusiasm from my heart as easily as I would pick an apple off a tree.

"Oh, Emily," J.T. whispered across the row to my niece as he punched his fist into the air. "I have been waiting for Uncle A.J. to start the research paper all year!"

"I know! I am so excited about this!" Emily replied as she swiveled her head toward her friend. "Ever since I was a young child growing up I imagined what it would be like to write a research paper with Uncle A.J.!"

As I looked around the classroom, I witnessed the unbridled enthusiasm of the class as they asked one another questions in an effort to predict how this entire adventure was going to proceed. The chattering consumed the early part of the class until Nick asked the first of so many important questions yet to come. "How many pages are we allowed to write? Will there be a limit?"

"Nick! What a fantastic question! I am loving this positive attitude! I had planned on limiting all of you to no more than twenty pages." That announcement quickly extinguished the fiery exuberance as everyone began to shake their heads, quietly generating a muffled rumble in the room. "Hey, people! What's up?" I needed to know what I had said to change the tenor of the room.

Chance raised his hand to proffer an explanation from his front seat near my desk. "Mr. Bucon, sir, you see, we were all at our study group last night actually talking about the research paper, and…" Chance stopped to look around for permission to continue. Johnny Mac, Shannon, Nick, and the rest of the class all nodded for him to proceed. "We know you don't want to stress us out and all, but we were kind of hoping to write a fifty-page paper which included thirty professional sources." They all leaned forward together, eagerly anticipating that my response would match their ultimate dream for a research paper.

I was stunned. What hard workers these students had become! I could not disappoint them. "Well, sure! Fifty pages it is! I love you guys!"

They all began to cheer from their desks as I slid into the swivel chair at my desk, clasped my hands behind my head, and leaned back to enjoy the moment. I closed my eyes as I realized just how wonderful life could be.

My Corner of the World

We teachers can dream, can't we? Life is never, I repeat, *never* what I just dreamed in any English classroom anywhere. The senior research project is a rite of passage for high school students everywhere. Yes, students are doing more research-based writing than ever in early grades, but the final hurdle of a completed lengthy paper is one which signals the preparedness of a young adult moving from high school to post-secondary education. The majority of students accept the challenge, overcoming any obstacles with ease, but others struggle with the confidence in themselves to meet the expectations of this project. Teachers become ringmasters at the circus, policemen in a traffic jam, or chefs in a five-star kitchen as we accept a group of students at all varying levels of ability and move them to a common ending point. The project itself becomes as much of a reflection on each student's capacity to write the paper as it is the teacher's skill set guiding them through the laborious endeavor.

I am familiar with the paths to success, I know my students' strengths and weaknesses, so I must confidently lead them to the research paper Promised Land. The class this year was a proving ground for me here at Central. I had taught an actual research class at Fike for the International Baccalaureate Programme and have guided thousands of senior English students through this process in my twenty years of teaching. With this being my first year at Central, I wanted to make sure I established a solid reputation for being able to navigate these waters.

My mission statement for this project has steadily grown to one of self-preservation for me as well as my students. I tell them our focus will be "low stress-high reward." The first part of the focus, the "low stress," simply means that as a group we will take the entire project slowly, making sure that everyone understands each stage before beginning the work. I express to them that "I am not going to drop this in your laps and ask you to do it on your own. I am with you every step of the way. I do need each one of you to give it your all on each step though." This honest conversation about breaking the project into smaller pieces removes the overwhelming nature of completing an entire project at once. Here is where the trust is established. The latter portion of our focus, the "high reward," is self-explanatory. If we keep the steps simple and do our best work at each stage of the process, the intrinsic reward will be the progressive development of self-confidence which culminates in a successfully completed paper. Young people are not unaware of their abilities and subsequent accomplishments; they know when they have done good work and when they have produced a mediocre or failing product.

This class had the choice of two possible papers. The first could build on the topic they chose as their Change Your World project, continuing the exploration of a current issue which they all found interesting. The second option was doing an in-depth comparison between two possible career options for them. As seniors who were heading off to college, many had never really explored these careers in detail so this was welcomed with open arms. The choices permitted them to follow their own thoughts and instincts, allowing them to make a stronger connection to their topic while providing ownership of the process itself.

My Corner of the World

The project would unfold over the course of several weeks. Nothing beats the tried and true method of doing the project itself. We established the parameters of the paper, setting out to complete ten pages in content with eight to ten various types of sources. We decided what questions we would want to answer for each topic choice. We discussed the evaluation of sources and whether or not certain ones were "good to use." We would argue occasionally about writing note cards. So many young people copy and paste content into papers to finish quickly without truly evaluating the context of the source or placement within the structure of their own paper. Note cards force students to write content, engaging it in a manner that simply reading or copying and pasting cannot guarantee. We outlined the content using the note cards, and, when finished, we were set to begin the writing of the actual paper. While this seems to be a simple practice, it is one during which each student can become more of an expert in the chosen topic than he or she was at the outset.

◆

Our weeks completing these stages had been a long road to travel, one during which some students struggled but maintained their focus while keeping their eyes on the ultimate prize. We were tired though, and, despite carefully completing each stage, we were all ready to finish this paper so we could move on with our lives. All of us just wanted to "get this thing done." Here was my dilemma: we had not yet reached the point at Central at which all of the students had their own Chrome Books. We were still somewhat technologically-challenged at the school with only one fully working computer lab. As a teacher I believe wholeheartedly in writing labs, particularly with class time set aside for writing. During this time I am able to circulate, spot check formatting and citation issues, do quick proofs, answer questions, and assess the progress of each student. Yes, many students have computers at home, but we had not reached the time of Google Docs, when work product remains in the cloud, easily accessed and updated from any computer.

With the idea of making a celebratory push to the finish line, I announced a week in advance that we would be having the first ever (and actual only ever) *Git 'Er Done, Knight*, a clever play on words based on Larry the Cable Guy's popular phrase and our school mascot. I chose one night when there would be no game or other school activity and told the kids I would be at school from 2:30 until 8:30, ready and willing to help anyone who wanted to "git 'er done" in one sitting after school.

"I am not staying at school that long! I am just doing it in class!" some would brazenly announce to me. "I mean, come on. Who wants to work after school that long on a research paper?" Some actually liked the idea, explaining to others that at least we could "stop starting and stopping the way we do every day in class."

I decided I needed to push back just a little bit if my plan were going to work. "Well, I am finished working on this in class now. We have spent a great deal of time starting these drafts in the lab this week. I am moving on to some other things, and besides, you all are *experts* writing this now. You are more than capable of doing this on your own whether it is at home or at the public library. You can do this."

The discussion continued as they talked among themselves, figuring out whether or not they were up for the challenge. "Do we *need* to be here at 2:30? I need to pick up my brother after school." "I have to work at six. Can I just come for a couple hours?" "I will be hungry by five!" I think they liked the idea of *Git 'Er Done, Knight*, but I needed to trust them to discover a way of making it work for them. It was their project, their paper, their time, and their decision.

"Can we order pizza or something?" J.T. asked.

"J.T., I will make a deal with you. If I can get an assurance from at least fifteen people to show up for the duration of the evening, I will find a way of getting pizza and drinks here for all of you."

"What about those of us who work?" someone yelled. "What if we cannot stay the entire time?"

"I totally understand and respect your honoring previous commitments. This is not about the pizza and drinks though. I just want to remove the concern about eating from your minds. The ultimate goal here is not a pizza party; the goal is to finish the paper. I cannot control anything beyond that. All I can say is that I will commit six hours of my time after a long day of school to be here with you to finish the paper."

At the end of class that day, I had well-over twenty *serious* commitments from the seniors to attend *Git 'Er Done, Knight*. They were not playing around here. I was not sure if it was the longer lab, the discontinuation of class time, or the offer of free pizza that won them over, but the reason did not make one bit of difference. I knew I could find some energy reserves to power through a six-hour writing lab, but I needed to figure out how to procure enough pizza and drinks for all of the kids who would be attending. At some point, I "mentioned" to my mom and my Aunt Lucille about what the students and I were doing that evening, and both of them agreed to split the cost of the pizza and drinks, even going so far as to deliver it all themselves. It looked as if *Git 'Er Done, Knight* was coming together.

♦

As soon as the final bell rang on the big day, I sprinted to the teacher's lounge, took off my tie, and changed my dress shoes for tennis shoes. I wanted to brace myself for what was going to be a long and productive night. On the way to the lounge I passed Luke, one of the quiet kids in class, as he carried his laptop down to my room. "It's OK if I do this on my laptop in your room, right? I just feel more comfortable working on this."

"Sure, Luke. Give me a few minutes to catch my breath then I will be down in the room to move the tables and desks around so we have more space." I was impressed with his eagerness but chuckled that this special night was already starting before I could even go to the bathroom. Luke was one of the guys who sat in the back with the other football players, and who, like so many other students, worried about his ability and at times struggled with the confidence to complete assignments. For Luke to attend so early and eager to work signaled that the night would be helpful to many of the students.

Luke helped me arrange the tables I had in my room as we set up surge protectors so that we could have work areas adjacent to the computer lab. We pushed desks over to the side for what eventually became a break area. As we worked to prepare the room, more people started showing up. Shannon slipped quietly through the doorway and asked if she could go ahead over to the lab to start working. Chance and

My Corner of the World

J.T. arrived shortly after Shannon, while some nonbelievers nonchalantly poked their heads into both rooms just to see who actually would show up. A couple of them asked if they could go home and come back a little later. "Do not let signing up stop you. We are open to anyone who wants to come!" I would tell anyone who would ask.

Within an hour students working on research papers populated my classroom and filled the computer lab. While friends like Emily and J.T. sat beside each other in my room at the table, others mixed more freely in the lab where they sat at the available desktops atop the four rows of tables. I bounced around as much as I could during the active lab, but I found it difficult to answer all the questions as quickly as my kids needed them answered. Eventually I would announce that I would begin sweeps through both rooms. "OK, everyone," I would say as I entered the lab. I am going to work down this row then back up the other one. If you have any questions before I make it to you, please ask a neighbor for some help. Remember that we can always address any issues later. Just type, people, and git 'er done!" Once I made it through one room, I would inform everyone that I was going next door to help their friends. We all became stronger as a class that evening as we depended more on one another, developing new levels of patience and understanding along the way, molding ourselves into the best kind of writing lab. Latecomers would arrive and eventually wedge themselves into spots vacated by people who had to leave. This corner of the school remained a beehive of activity throughout the afternoon and early evening until we eventually stopped at the halfway point for some much needed pizza and pop.

"OK, everyone! Make sure you save your work. It is time for a break. I am going to run downstairs to pick up the pizza. The pop is already in the room across the hallway." Everyone took a deep breath, finished the section on which they were working, then saved their papers as I made my way downstairs to pick up the eight boxes of pizza Mom and Aunt Lou had donated. When I returned upstairs, the room was full of kids excitedly talking about how much they had accomplished so far and making plans to have this entire paper finished before they left. They cheered in disbelief at the amount of pizza I carried with me when I entered the room, some rushing to grab their slices. "Whoa! Whoa! Whoa!" I begged them off. "Could we possibly have someone lead a prayer before we eat?" Once the prayer was finished, the girls picked out their slices first then the guys followed for their turn. We all sat around to talk for a while, continuing the conversation about their progress before veering off into typical teenage topics which had to be edited slightly since I was in the room. Eventually people began to clean up so they could head back over to the work areas to finish what they had started while I stayed to straighten out the room before returning to the circulation routine we had established earlier that afternoon.

I was back in the computer lab when I heard a loud sob originating from the classroom next door. I did not think much of it until J.T. and Emily slowly walked into the lab and pulled me aside. "Uncle A.J., something happened over in your room," Emily began, looking to J.T. to finish the story.

"What's wrong?" I asked as I looked for an answer between the two of them. "Just tell me. I won't be angry."

J.T. looked at Emily then back at me, "Luke lost everything. His computer shut down, and he cannot find his paper anywhere."

"Well, that's not good. He can't have *lost* it though!" I slowly walked over to class as I wanted to be the calm adult in the room. Luke had his head in his hands, leaning forward, staring at his laptop. Everyone around him was quietly watching Luke, worried about whether or not this was actually true and possibly grateful that it was not happening to them. He was inarticulately mumbling to himself something about "saving" and "a disaster."

I slid a chair close to him and whispered, "Luke? Can you tell me what happened? Maybe I can help."

Luke sat up, took a deep breath, and offered the laptop to me with his hands. "I don't know. I mean, I was typing then my laptop just shut off. I turned it back on, and now I can't find the paper."

"Luke, did you not save it?" I carefully asked.

"I thought I did, but I don't think so. I honestly can't remember."

I looked through all of his files and struggled to find anything resembling a paper. There were no unnamed files and no versions tucked away anywhere. The two of us searched and searched, but any work Luke completed appeared to have vanished. Luke was now at a point at which he was completely dejected about the project and appeared to doubt his ability to even finish.

I asked him to give me one minute during which I talked to both sides of our writing lab to tell them what happened and that they should say a prayer or two to help Luke regroup. I told them that I was going to need an extended amount of time to work with him as I knew he would need my undivided attention to pull himself out of this.

"OK, Luke. I am going to be here by your side through this. Sometimes stuff like this happens in life. We think we are moving along, and everything is fine then *Bam!,* we are blindsided and end up picking up the pieces. I have been there, Luke, and this is my advice to you: shake it off, buckle down, and start all over. The longer you think about it, the more time you allow doubt to creep into your head."

Luke shook his head, "OK, Mr. Bucon. What do we do?"

Together we resorted his note cards according to his outline, putting the ones he needed at the beginning of his paper on top. We opened up a new document, naming it as we saved it. Together we wrote the first paragraph, made sure Luke was formatting everything correctly, then we saved the document. We continued this process, moving to the second paragraph and then the third paragraph, continuously saving. Eventually Luke remembered writing all of this before but noticed that it actually seemed to sound better now. After less than an hour, Luke said he was confident to continue on his own and no longer needed me at his side. I eventually left him to complete as much work as he could before 8:30 and went back to helping the rest of the class, a class which apparently no longer needed my help as one by one they put the final touches on their papers. My night became easier after that, moving around from student to student, not answering nearly as many questions as they all became the experts at writing these papers that they were destined to be.

The *Git 'Er Done, Knight* was a success in more ways than I could have imagined. Most of the students had little difficulty completing the revisions on their papers and developed that confidence they needed to complete the numerous ones they would write in college on their own. Students like Luke discovered a sense of accomplishment for having overcome setbacks in this process, learning that no obstacles are too difficult to overcome if we rely on one another and believe in our own ability to rise above challenges. Honestly, I have never experienced the dream of an eager class which writes a fifty-page paper with thirty resources of their own accord. As I said, these classes just do not exist in my world, and I am perfectly fine with that. I enjoyed the reality of a group of students who believed in "low stress-high reward," a group of students who instinctively came to the aid of one another, a group of students who worked hard without making excuses, and a group of students who just wanted to git 'er done.

14

Seeds

The quietness and solitude of the library had long since replaced the chaos of my students moving the furniture to make way for our makeshift theater. The guys had carried the longer tables back between the three long rows of bookcases where no student had walked for over a year. The girls had arranged the chairs into two sections facing the area which would serve as our stage, a small section directly beside the book check-out area. An HD television sat atop a multimedia cart centered between a podium and polished side table with three empty ominous chairs closer to the front than the audience would be sitting. The quietness and solitude was the deep breath for moments which were to begin the next day.

I stood near a back row of four tables pushed together into a slight crescent shape. The tables were draped with maroon outdoor tablecloths and adorned with tiny pots of red plastic flowers Mom found for us at Dollar General. The multicolored scrapfolios with their numerous creative designs were opened to a variety of pages, all representing the unique aspects of my students' reflections over the past year. Each opened a window to a different story, each offered a distinctive view of every single student, and each would soon become an opportunity to share a moment that many would not soon forget.

♦

The remainder of the school year went by rather quickly, particularly for the seniors who were rightfully anticipating graduation and anxious for the next stage in their lives to commence. Holding onto the reins of any class at the end of the year is always a challenge, but as a teacher of seniors, the struggle can be more precarious. Underclassmen are ready to leave for the summer, but seniors are racing to leave for the rest of their lives. Still, I wanted to end the year connecting the dots in the past to the moments in the here and now. The year had been a unique journey of sorts for all of us, particularly this special class of seniors about to graduate.

A month or so outside of graduation day, the students relished the idea of putting the final touches on their scrapfolios. They slipped completed research papers into empty sleeves adjacent to pages about the spring musical, the senior showcase, spring sports, and prom. Many added student choice pages about friends and family as well. I asked them to create an exit page, one which we would call our "Past, Present, and Future" page. Here each student would include a recent picture or one from his or her childhood. I wanted a reflection on this point in their lives, one which would never come again, one during which change would affect each student in different ways. They needed to go back to consider who they were years ago; they could decide if it would be four years, eight years, or even more than that. Who were they back then?

What were their aspirations? Who were their heroes? What were their greatest challenges? They also had to contemplate who they were now. What accomplishments had they experienced in their lives? What obstacles had they overcome? Who were the family members who had helped them to this pivotal moment in their lives? What fond memories do they have of friends, teachers, coaches, and school? Who are the people they had lost in their lives? They had to consider their future as well. What were their immediate plans? Where did they see themselves four years from now? What values, qualities, or skills would help them to be successful? This was not a questionnaire; I was asking them to dig deep into the thoughts and feelings that were swirling around inside of them, the ones that made graduation the mish-mash of emotional and mental turmoil it is for many students and families.

One day early in the process we took a break from working on the scrapfolio to discuss the upcoming final event of the year for us. As they all sat and listened to my explanation, I shared how much I had enjoyed the year. I offered my appreciation for all of their hard work and understanding when they did not always "see" the final destination. "We are here now, everyone. I remember how great those presentations were at midterm. You shared some wonderful aspects of your lives, and we all learned a great deal about one another."

"Oh, yeah, Bucon," Mason interrupted. "Didn't you say that maybe we could do that again for the final exam as well?"

"Well, yes. I did say something like that, but I am going to put out a final challenge to all of you to do something that no one here has done. I mean, this is going to be so cool!" I now laughed at their eye rolls and groans, choosing to believe they had become signs of love and respect rather than student apathy and pretentiousness. After giving them a moment to express their senior displeasure with the world, I chuckled and continued, writing dates on the board underneath the title: Commencement Presentations.

Emily squinted with skepticism. "What *is* that? What is a Commencement Presentation?"

"Oh, it is really nothing that different from what you did earlier this year with your scrapfolio presentations. I am just adding a couple wrinkles to those presentations. Seriously, that's all."

"Like what?" Nick asked.

"Well, first of all, I am going to extend the time frame a little bit. I expect these presentations to be five to seven minutes."

"Five to seven minutes?" some of them began muttering. "Do we have to do the entire scrapfolio?" "What will we say?"

"This will be so easy! You have everything right in front of you. You will have three elements to present. The first element is your research paper." I stopped to look around. "No, you will not read it. I just want you to talk about your reasons for choosing the topic you did, the highlights of your research, and your conclusion. That's all." I felt the shade they were throwing at me. *We are ready to graduate, yet this guy wants us to go back and talk about our research paper again?* "OK, I know you are not thrilled with this, but here is why I want to do this. Back in North Carolina, all of our seniors had to do a presentation on their senior project or they would not graduate. They hated it as well, but these same students soon discovered that colleges and universities were expecting them to be competent doing formal presentations of content from their courses. I am telling you now as I told my students in North Carolina—this will help you to be successful in the future."

J.T. nodded then continued, "OK. That *is* easy, everyone. Come on. What are the other two elements, Uncle A.J.?"

"Thanks, J.T. The second element is something you have already had practice doing. Pick any two or three of your scrapfolio pages and share them with the audience. The third element is simply your exit page, the one you are writing now. See? This is no big deal. Two minutes on your research paper. Two minutes on your scrapfolio pages. Two minutes on your exit page. You've got this!"

As they seemed to be settling in to this concept, someone asked, "How are we going to have time to fit everyone in? There are a bunch of people going."

"If you look up here at the board, I have an entire week set aside. Tomorrow we will have a drawing so you can choose the day on which you want to go."

"So we just hold up the scrapfolio and tell the class about it the way we did at midterms?" Emily asked, being a little more open-minded herself now. "That's easy."

"Well, I am not quite done, Emily. You are going to create a PowerPoint presentation for each element, and we will have it showing on a TV. You will take pictures of the scrapfolio pages you will present. Having something special for the audience and the *evaluators* to see is important."

"Whoa! Stop!" Chance bellowed from the back of the room. "Evaluators? What do you mean by that? Aren't you grading us?"

"Well, yes and no." I began, knowing that I was heading into the rough part of this assignment. "I have made arrangements to have a small panel of judges sitting in the front to rate your presentation and to ask you questions."

The grumbling really began. I felt as if I had taken lunch money from the younger sibling of the biggest bully in school. "Evaluators?" *Sharp stares.* "Who are they? They don't know us!" *Shaking heads.* "You're crazy." *Slamming books.* "What kinds of questions?"

I wanted to be as serious as possible in case they thought I was playing some kind of insensitive joke. I looked at poor Shannon, poor quiet Shannon, who appeared on the verge of breaking down along with half a dozen other people in the room. "Look, you will be fine. We have always been about accepting challenges in this class and here at Central. We always dig deep to find a little more inside of us than we thought we had. I would never ask you to do something that I did not believe in my heart that you could do."

"Who are some of the evaluators?" Chance asked, much more calmly than I would have anticipated.

"Well, Mr. Volpe, my English teacher when I was a student, has agreed to come. I think Father Dennis and Father McSweeney are coming as well. And Doc…"

"Doc is coming?" Chance asked, perking up with a touch of enthusiasm. Doctor Joseph Viglietta had been my principal at Central when I graduated and had been their principal when this class entered as freshmen, retiring following their sophomore year after a long tenure as principal at Central. He was a beloved man and had been a difficult leader to replace. "Doc is really coming?"

"I have spoken to him and given him the dates. He is looking at his calendar and has promised to be here at least one of the days on the board. He is a busy man, Chance."

Everyone's attitude changed after my explanation and the announcement of some of the guests. They settled back into the trust we had established throughout the year and began to talk about what they would say, who they hoped would be their evaluators, and all sorts of other crazy teenager stuff.

"Can we get dressed up?" Emily asked. "I think we should be allowed to dress up instead of wearing these stupid uniforms."

"You know, Emily, I do not think Mrs. Sancomb will have a problem with that at all." The class appeared content with all that we had discussed and continued talking among themselves. "Everyone, I did have one last item to mention though." I chuckled nervously then cleared my throat. "I am going to be contacting everyone's parents either by email or phone to tell them your presentation date and time. I think it is important for them to have an opportunity to see you do your Commencement Presentation."

Silence, the eternal kind.

The grumbling renewed. Why do I do this to myself? "Our parents?" "I don't want them to hear this!" *Puffing nostrils*. "Why do they need to be here?" "They see us all the time!" *Clenched jaws*. "You're crazy." *Crossed arms*. "When is this class over? When is graduation?"

A.J. Bucon

These kids. How could I not love them?

◆

A calmness with an underlying excitement slowly developed throughout my class as preparation for this final event continued. Everyone worked in Room 301, painstakingly finishing their scrapfolios then moving to the adjacent computer lab to begin developing their PowerPoint presentations. Their last days befitted this class as groups conversed enthusiastically about the intricate details of what they were planning while others huddled together, finding kindred spirits in their concerns of speaking in front of the evaluators, classmates, and family members who chose to attend. I was blessed with a wonderful opportunity to sit down with each student individually as they prepared. The remaining class periods afforded me an opportunity to allay any fears, support creative ideas, and provide technical support for troubled PowerPoint presentations. More importantly though, I was able to spend quality personal time with each student I had grown to appreciate over the course of the past year.

As the time wound down toward the first day of presentations, everyone pitched in where they could. The class gathered in the library where all of the tables and chairs needed to be moved then wiped clear of any dust and dirt before the guests would arrive. We rolled in the multimedia cart so that everyone could have an opportunity to practice; those truly nervous students took a little more time, even coming upstairs during lunch to practice with one another. Each person insisted on seeing the guest list in order to confirm their parents and family were coming and to discover on which day Doc would be there to evaluate them. The entire prologue to the Commencement Presentations became a wave of excitement for the students as well as their teacher.

Each day of the presentations was a new experience. A new set of evaluators would arrive for our class period, different sets of parents, grandparents, and siblings would be welcomed by the warm smile of a student who several weeks ago might not have even wanted them there, and each day the unexpected would happen as every single senior took his or her place behind the podium, grabbed the handheld mouse to advance the PowerPoint slideshow, then allowed themselves to be vulnerable to the audience. Questions from the evaluators followed each presentation, questions that came from the evaluators' own curiosity regarding what the students had shared about their research project, their scrapfolio pages, and even their plans for the future. Each student handled the pressure with maturity and poise as they responded to the numerous questions and showed the entire gathering how prepared they were for this moment, how prepared they were to accept similar challenges after graduation.

Beyond the quality of the presentations rested the transparency of all of the students who chose to provide not only remarkable understandings of their research topics but also genuine insights into who they were as individuals. Many used the gratitude page as a means to express an awareness of those who had influenced them. Many students chose to thank the parents in attendance and even those who were not able to attend by using a parent scrapfolio page to frame the importance of their guidance, support, and love. A few students had lost parents earlier in their lives and tearfully recognized a mother or father who had nobly weathered the storm of single parenthood. Colorful student choice pages featuring their memories playing football, basketball, baseball, and other sports going as far back as grade school teams served as springboards for teammate recognition. Senior athletes offered emotional acknowledgement of the hard work, leadership, and inspiration of coaches who had molded them into accomplished athletes. The exit pages presented a vehicle for a final transitory declaration of each student's past and a hope-filled glimpse into their future. All took the opportunity to close their presentations noting the importance of attending a school like Central, the privilege of learning from teachers dedicated to making all of them better people, and growing as part of a close community of friends and family.

By the time the entire class had finished, the students and I were emotionally exhausted. While this seems so strange to say, particularly for what many outsiders would consider a simple presentation, we had all invested so much of ourselves into these individual testimonies. We had left our hearts open to the voices of others and found a commonality despite the diverse parts of our lives we chose to discuss. We had not anticipated the honesty and vulnerability each and every student exhibited as each took his or her turn in the spotlight. We did not anticipate the connections we had made with one another not only this year but in the years which preceded it.

As a teacher I want to plant seeds in my students' lives that will grow as my students mature. In their hearts all teachers want to plant seeds that are not just about the lectures we deliver, the homework we assign, the projects we require, or the tests we administer; we want our students to take with them more than just the subject matter because in the end much of that content will fade as students acquire new knowledge, instinctively keeping only that which will continue to remain purposeful in their lives. We also want to plant seeds that reflect the values and beliefs we have and seeds that will continue to develop as skills we see as important to the future success of our students. In life as well, we all plant seeds as individual people when we make choices that affect not only ourselves but others. We choose how we interact in our relationships. We decide how we teach our children values through our behavior. We elect to make a difference in our place of work, in our churches, in our local communities, and in our cities. These choices are our seeds, the ways in which we make our corners of the world a better place. Throughout the year I had hoped that the seeds we planted together as a class would eventually grow into something much larger in the lives of my students. There was a convergence of sorts during this week of Commencement Presentations, one in which all of the seeds we had planted bloomed much sooner than any of us expected.

15

Into the Reflecting Pool

As I walked down the steps toward the Class of 2013's graduation procession line outside the Oglebay Park Amphitheater, I felt as if I had been here at least more than one time in my life. The familiar feeling reached back years to when I was a graduate from Central Catholic High School, traversed the five hundred miles and twenty years I had spent as a teacher at Fike High School in North Carolina, and finally returned back here where I am a teacher at my alma mater. I would say that it was not so much the locations that were sparking a sense of reminiscence but the event itself, the energy and excitement generated by change, transition, and graduation.

I have so few memories from my graduation day from Central. I do recall having it here at the amphitheater, a tradition that has clearly dated back farther than my memory will allow. I am positive we wore the same maroon and white graduation gowns and caps that the class wore today. Family and guests sat around us in the amphitheater where we all anxiously awaited for names to be called to receive the much-desired diplomas. However, there was one guest missing today, one which caused much distress to many of my class: the cicadas. These inch-long insects arrive every seventeen years and had chosen our graduation time to be in full force, feeding on the small branches of trees, singing their loud songs, flying into girls' hair and onto our clothing, being generally harmless yet annoying pests.

As a class we were undeterred. That diploma was ours, and we were willing to wade through the countless hordes of black insects, swatting them back to the trees, stomping on them, and laughing away our fears just to have Doctor Viglietta place that maroon folder in our grubby hands as we marched across the stage. I can recall Doc announcing the names of my classmates, I can recall my own walk up the stairs to the stage, and I can recall sitting back down to read the contents of the diploma. That is it though. I do not remember any speeches or any celebrations after the ceremony as we all exited the amphitheater. I was ready to go. Life awaited me, and I was anxious to see what the world had ready to offer.

Nearly seven years later as a teacher in North Carolina, I had become a different part of the celebration, and I experienced it with emotions unlike those of the students or family members. I remember working with Lynn Barnes, a math teacher at Fike who was also in charge of graduation in the huge auditorium of our school. The practices! The interminable practices! The experience of organizing two hundred-plus seniors in alphabetical order, keeping them in two separate processional lines, and sternly discouraging them from talking became an annual event in my life. Lynn would guide them from the podium on the stage, patiently explaining the order and timing of graduation while the handful of remaining teachers on the graduation committee would patrol the aisles ready to pounce on those students who became too talkative or playful. At times it was a tedious process, but we always found a way of keeping them focused. By the time the practices and the graduation day procession into Fike's auditorium were over, I would sit with Felissa in the back row where I would collapse into a chair she had saved for me, another year in the books.

Despite the unpleasantness of the repetitive and time-consuming Fike High School graduation practices, I discovered I had an inner joy for this process, particularly on graduation day itself. On this day, everyone looked their best and felt so proud to eventually walk across that stage. As a teacher to so many of these students, I had a vested interest in their success and had made personal connections with so many of them. I had been a quiet passenger, a helpful navigator, and even an annoying back-seat driver to many of my students that graduation, their passage from this stage of their lives to the next, was a bittersweet point in my life. So as I walked up and down the lines prior to the procession while checking for unbuttoned top buttons and offering a plastic cup in which to spit gum, I embraced the best part of this moment, the opportunity I had to talk to each student individually and to share a final smile and precursory congratulations on this day of endings and new beginnings.

On a whim, I bought a blue seersucker jacket for Central's graduation in 2013. I have never worn anything like this in my entire life, but I just felt especially right in it. I felt as if I had shuffled off my exterior of a person who at times doubted the changes he had made in his life, becoming someone with a renewed confidence and outlook. I spent an hour tying my new bow tie then slapped on some sunglasses to embrace the conclusion of my first year at Central. This year had been a reaffirmation of who I was as a person, as a native son, and as a teacher. I embraced the change in me as I felt the warmth of the spring sun rising that morning for graduation.

Free from a checklist of students or a plastic cup for gum, I wound my way through the senior class, stopping to enjoy the moment with young people who had welcomed me into their lives that year, their senior year. The gathering of students was a place for countless pictures, hugs, handshakes, and words of appreciation from all sides. The liveliness of this group only decreased in volume as the time came for the procession when the seniors calmly fell back into line, adjusted their gowns, and confirmed the tassels were draped to the right side. Business as usual for this group.

Two rows of faculty led the graduates down the steps into Oglebay Park's sunken garden, a serene area with blossoming trees lining the outer edges of the beautifully manicured green grass which surrounded a rectangular reflecting pool. Near the exit at the opposite end more steps served as the entrance to the amphitheater itself. The procession atop the edging sidewalks of the sunken garden continued to quiet both groups as the tone changed from the anticipatory enthusiasm of the staging area to a ceremonial focus which signaled the importance of the moment at hand. As my line traveled closer to the steps to the amphitheater, I gazed into the reflecting pool. The clarity of the water and the soft blue paint of the inner cement generated a shimmering gleam atop the still water of the pool—a silent oasis in the midst of the hundred people walking beside it. The perfection of the pool lent our moment a solemnity fittingly appropriate for its intended purpose, one of reflection.

The descent from the top of the amphitheater steps to the stage took us down through the family, friends, and guests who filled the ascending rows of benches beneath the outstretched limbs of an even larger collection of trees which shaded the left and right seating areas of the amphitheater. This left the graduates a spot so sunny that they all wore sunglasses to keep the bright sun from their eyes throughout the commencement ceremony. The faculty found their seats on the stage where we had been placed behind the dignitaries in attendance: Monsignor Ostrowski, several parish priests, the school board president, and the guest speaker. Once the last person in each group had found his or her seat, we waited for Principal Becky Sancomb to welcome everyone to the moment all in attendance had anxiously awaited.

The graduation program itself was quite surreal for me in this setting. Decades ago I sat where Emily and her classmates sat, a member of the Class of 1982 fading in and out amidst the words of numerous speakers that morning. The two days were strikingly similar as I contemplated the conflux of my past and present, seeing myself as both a high school graduate and the teacher of those about to walk across the stage. Both people were me, both were sitting there at the completion of a remarkable period of time, both had overcome struggles that life had presented, and both had witnessed the joys that every single day can bring. The graduate and the teacher both stood on the precipice of his future, unsure of where the road would take him, uncertain if he was prepared for its twists and turns, yet confident that his faith in himself would take him where he wanted to go.

The presentation of diplomas began as Becky called out each graduate's name who, in turn, would proceed in a restrained pace onto the stage where the graduate would shake Monsignor Ostrowski's hand then receive the reward for all of his or her accomplishments. "Emily Elizabeth Bucon," Becky announced with a slight smile in the corner of her mouth, slowly turning back toward the seat where I no longer sat. I moved to the diploma table to retrieve Emily's diploma. She smiled as she climbed the steps to meet me where I gave her a congratulatory hug. Her friends let out a collective "Awwww!" when I gave Emily the diploma, making it difficult for both of us not to laugh as we rolled our eyes and shook our heads when the photographer took our picture from below the stage.

Monsignor Ostrowski concluded the long ceremony with his final benediction. Shortly thereafter, the thumping wonder of "Pomp and Circumstance" accompanied the graduates as they ascended the concrete steps out of the amphitheater. Once the last graduate left his row, Becky changed the music from the classical to the modern with the student-chosen "Happy" by Pharrell Williams generating an explosion of cheers from the grads. I turned and said my goodbyes to my fellow teachers then proceeded to climb the steps myself where I began to mingle with departing parents, many of whom shared their appreciation for all that I had done that year for their children. Upon reaching the sunken gardens, I discovered the quiet serenity of the reflecting pool drastically disturbed.

My Corner of the World

These newly graduated teenagers with white and maroon robes were frolicking in the two-foot deep reflecting pool, splashing one another while laughing and cheering. Parents stood watching the lively chaos, snapping pictures and pointing fingers while beaming as we all bore witness to the sight in front of us, the sight of a group of individuals washing away some of who they were in order to become who they were destined to be. Many graduates hopped out of the pool to take soaked pictures with their friends and families only to return shortly thereafter to reenter the pool where they would continue to hug one another for one last time before leaving for towels, dry clothes, graduation parties, and their futures.

As the graduates, the parents, the brothers and sisters, the friends, the teachers, and the random guests eventually dispersed, the reflecting pool regained its original tranquility while not losing any of the pristine sparkle the water had prior to the commencement program. Once again, any random traveler could walk through the sunken garden to stop for a moment beside the pool to revisit the past and consider the future while gazing at his or her own reflection in the water. The only elapse of time would be the shifting shadows of overhanging trees or the fading twitter of birds flying away to adjacent hills. The still water would always await a slight sweep of a traveler's hand which would swirl the reflection floating there, erasing that image forever but eventually revealing a new person who would walk away into a corner of the world which would be defined by personal choices, a sense of clear vision, and an unquestionable belief in self and others.

ACKNOWLEDGEMENTS

Thanks again to Jodi Anthony Proietti, Betsy Knorr, Becky Sancomb, Kathy Proctor, and the Class of 2013.

I am indebted to my beta-readers: my niece Emily Bucon, my neighbors Chris and John Hannig, my dear friend Jodi Anthony Proietti, and *my* high school English teacher Lou Volpe. All of your suggestions and insights helped carry *My Corner of the World* to the finish line.

I also want to truly thank the countless people who have read my blog *Time and Space*. Your kind words, texts, and emails to me about the influence my posts have had in your lives helped nurture the voice in me to grow in confidence.

I have had so many colleagues throughout my teaching career at both Ralph L. Fike High School and Central Catholic High School. For your love, support, and influence I am eternally grateful.

Thank you to my mom and my entire family both in Wheeling and Wilson. I love all of you.

A REQUEST TO THE READER

If you enjoyed reading *My Corner of the World*, I would truly appreciate any review you could write. I am offering the book primarily on Amazon so a review posted there would benefit me as an independent publisher. If you did not secure the book from Amazon, please feel free to send any comments to my webpage at www.ajbucon.com. Thank you so much for your support.

PHOTO AND PRINT CREDIT

Bucon, A.J. "Table and Chairs." 500 MILE PRESS, 2018.

Johnson, Spencer. *Who Moved My Cheese?* G P Putnam, 1998.

Proietti, Jodi Anthony. "Savannah Wall." 2018.

"Ripped, Paper, Legal Pad." *Pixabay.com*, pixabay.com/en/ripped-paper-legal-pad-ripped-paper-1806471

About the Author

 A.J. Bucon grew up in Wheeling, West Virginia, where he graduated from Central Catholic High School in 1982. A.J. graduated from West Liberty State College in 1986. He moved to Wilson, North Carolina, where he taught for 21 years at Ralph L. Fike High School before returning to his alma mater in 2012.

A.J. has earned numerous accolades throughout his numerous years in education. He has been a National Board Certified teacher since 2011 and was recognized as Wilson County Schools Teacher of the Year in 2001, WTVD11 Neighborhood Hero – Educator of the Year in 2002, and The Bonnie McKeever Roberts Award for Excellence in Education in 2016.

A.J. is currently teaching English at Central Catholic High School. He continues to make regular posts on his blog *Time and Space*. *My Corner of the World* is his first foray into book writing.

A.J. currently resides in Wheeling, West Virginia, and makes regular visits to see his son Robert who continues to reside in Wilson, North Carolina, with his wife Emily and two children, Justin and Kaylee.

Social Media

Blog: *Time and Space* www.ajbucon.com
Twitter: AJ Bucon @bucon_aj

www.ingramcontent.com/pod-product-compliance
Lightning Source LLC
Chambersburg PA
CBHW020254030426
42336CB00010B/757